COMING ATTRACTIONS?

COMING ATTRACTIONS?

Hollywood, High Tech,
and the Future of Entertainment

Philip E. Meza

STANFORD BUSINESS BOOKS
An Imprint of Stanford University Press
Stanford, California
2007

Stanford University Press
Stanford, California

Library of Congress Cataloging-in-Publication Data

Meza, Philip E.
  Coming attractions? : Hollywood, high tech, and the future of entertainment / Philip E. Meza.
     p. cm.
  Includes bibliographical references and index.
  ISBN-13: 978-0-8047-5660-0 (cloth : alk. paper)
  1. Mass media and technology--United States--History. 2. Mass media--Economic aspects--United States--History. I. Title.

P96.T422U636 2007
302.23--dc22
                                        2006039694

Designed by Bruce Lundquist
Typeset at Stanford University Press in 10/14 Minion

To my wife Marjorie and my family

CONTENTS

ACKNOWLEDGMENTS

THIS BOOK WAS INSPIRED BY my work with Andy Grove and Robert A. Burgelman at the Stanford Graduate School of Business. I was lucky to begin working with them in 1999. Just as playing tennis with excellent partners will improve one's game, working with these two world-class pros has greatly improved my thinking on the issues discussed in this book. I am deeply indebted to both of them.

Thanks also go to Haim Mendelson at Stanford for his advice and guidance concerning this book and other projects, to Martha Cooley, my editor at SUP, for her invaluable help making a manuscript into a book, to Alan Harvey, SUP's Editor-in-Chief, who deftly picked up where Martha left off, and to David Horne, for superb copyediting. I appreciate the help and encouragement concerning this book that I received from Les Vadasz, former president of Intel Capital, who has first-hand experience with the power triumvirate of Silicon Valley-Hollywood-Washington, D.C. I also want to thank Amanda Marks and Tom Sturges, two very knowledgeable and thoughtful record company executives who shared their views with me, and Tivo cofounder Michael Ramsay for an insightful interview.

The M.B.A. students at Stanford whom I have worked with over the years have added to my understanding of this material. Special thanks are due to former students Benjamin Cha, Lewis Fanger, Cecilia Goytisolo O'Reilly, and Kausik Rajgopal, who wrote cases that help inform parts of this book. In addition, Reuben Chen, formerly of the Stanford Law School, provided valuable contributions to a note I coauthored on intellectual property, some of which is reflected in this book.

Several clever friends of mine deserve mention for their help with this project. Scientist and entrepreneur Tom Annau and former professor and researcher Jim Oliver reviewed the manuscript early in the process and made valuable suggestions. I am grateful to both of them. Filmmaker Paul Aldridge and executive Karen Leigh also read and commented on early drafts, making helpful suggestions. Former naval aviator and executive Jack Bland suggested very clever titles. I also want to thank the three anonymous reviewers who offered thoughtful comments on the manuscript of this book.

Most of the books and journals (even obscure ones) I used to research this book were obtained through the outstanding San Francisco Public Library (particularly the Main and Marina branches), which along with librarian extraordinaire Ralph Thompson deserve a note of thanks.

Finally, and most important, I want to extend my personal gratitude to those whom I owe the most: my wife Marjorie, who encouraged me to write this book, and my family, Edward, Grace, Robert, Sara, Robbie, Juliana, Caitlin, Kristen, and Scarlett, who have always been supportive of me and each other.

San Francisco, California

COMING ATTRACTIONS?

1 INTRODUCTION

WATCHING A MOVIE OR A TELEVISION PROGRAM on your iPod is more than just cool. It represents the latest step in the coming together of several streams of development, in both technologies and ways of doing business. This convergence can offer challenging but profitable opportunities for content companies and technology companies to serve consumers and make money in new ways. For companies that are unprepared, it will be Moore's Law meets Murphy's Law. This is because the new technologies are more powerful than the old technologies, and the new technologies are more impatient. They are impatient in that the new (or newly combined) technologies discussed in this book break down the boundaries that separated old technologies and old forms of content and greatly reduce the need for the costly physical assets necessary to be a movie studio or distributor, a television broadcaster, or a record company. This can put more power in more hands or, conversely, multiply the power of consolidating media giants.

Until now, most content and technologies have kept an arm's length from each other. Even when content companies and technology companies were owned by the same parent company, usually they did not work well together or anticipate each other's trajectories well. This will have to change. Because the technologies that will govern the way content is created, distributed, and consumed are changing, more than ever it is crucial that content and technology get to understand each other; in a phrase, get in bed together.

Strange bedfellows may be fun in theory, but can be very difficult to manage in practice, if only because the partners know so little about each other: their interests, goals, and true intentions. While there may be parallels to other aspects of life, this has been particularly true at the intersection where technological change affects existing business models. In particular, some information industries, such as those producing music, movies, and television shows, have been especially uncomfortable at this intersection.

It may seem odd to think of music, movies, and television shows as the product of "information industries," but that is what they are: they are audio and visual information. This information is often referred to as "content." For the past hundred years the products (content) of these industries were consumed separately. Music was about records, movies were about celluloid film, and television was about images broadcast over the air or delivered via cable. As we will see, the intersections of technological change and existing business models proved upsetting to the content owners even when they were still distinct industries. This may be surprising given that these industries themselves were created from technological innovations. But instead of welcoming the change, these industries often tried to strangle the new technologies in their cradles, usually by hiring lawyers or lobbying legislators to put their hands around the young necks.

It's a funny story though: in the end, the industries ended up benefiting from the technological change. It created new channels and new ways for consumers to consume content. Content owners thought the sky was falling, but instead it often rained money. This was because the technologies eventually developed into new and profitable channels for delivering content. Think of how the phonograph and later the compact disc (CD) presented new opportunities to consume music; television and the videocassette recorder (VCR) for consuming movies; and now the iPod and the next device to come down the street for consuming anything that can be digitized.

If content owners were fearful of technological change in the past, well then something truly terrifying to them is coming their way: converged digital technology for entertainment. These industries used to be distinct, their products consumed separately with separate equipment that gave separate experiences, and often governed by the familiar economic forces such as economies of scope and scale. Nowadays, they are becoming less distinct. This loss of distinction in the way content is consumed (and created) is often called *convergence.* Content is becoming more like data, and data are governed by a whole different set of forces. These forces are far more powerful and move at far faster rates than those that governed audio and visual information in the past. These are the same forces that governed digital computing; the forces that put the processing power of a computer the size of your living room in 1970 into a notebook computer today. (See Appendix A for a discussion of the most important forces.)

Facing another new intersection of technological change and established business models, content owners are again scared. This time, they have good reason to be nervous. This book will show how in the past, technology change ended up altering the environment to the benefit of content owners. Today, the same opportunities for technological changes to benefit content owners exist, but there is less room to get it wrong initially. Analog was patient; digital is as impatient as it is powerful.

COMPLEMENTS IN COMPETITORS' CLOTHING

Lately, movie and television studios and recording companies (let's think of these as Hollywood) have found themselves at odds with technology companies, such as computer companies, microprocessor makers and makers of networking gear (Silicon Valley for short), and even phone and cable companies. These different industries—entertainment and computing and telecommunications—are complements: each makes the other more valuable. Think about the boon that digitization in the 1980s represented to the recording industry, which suddenly found new jugs, that is, compact discs, for the old wine of its back catalog of music, or the value of computer technology in the 1990s to movies, especially the digital animation of the *Toy Story* films or *Finding Nemo,* done completely by computers. The two industries need each other and make each other better. However, relations between these two industries have become chilly if not downright hostile. Former Disney CEO Michael Eisner once compared computer and microprocessor companies to "sword suppliers for pirates."[1] Technology company executives have been similarly unkind about what they perceive as the Luddite tendencies of entertainment companies in their efforts to slow down one of the most exciting and important (and critical to the financial health of technology companies) applications of technology: digital distribution of content.

However, it is not just entertainment and technology company executives and investors who have a stake in the way these strange bedfellows get along.

We all do. Over the past decade, content owners—the movie and television studios, recording companies, and others who produce so much popular intellectual property (IP)—have felt themselves at increasing risk of theft. They think, with some justification, that they are losing billions of dollars through piracy. At the behest of these content owners, laws are being enacted by the United States Congress to protect copyright holders from technological change that can affect the way we consume the products of these companies, now and in the future. Some of these changes may be justified; some may be unnecessary, in their most benign form, or even harmful in the most malign forms. Imagine if the United States Supreme Court had outlawed the VCR, as it nearly did in 1984 at the behest of movie studios (it avoided doing this by one vote): it would have saved studios from a new technology that created a new market that now accounts for around 60 percent of their gross domestic annual revenue.[2]

This book deals with owning, distributing, and getting paid for information. This information can take many forms, for example, a song or a movie, and be expressed as a series of zeros and ones—that is to say, digitized. Even before the advent of digitization, before computers networked to the Internet made swapping songs and other forms of digitized information easy, content owners had difficulties adjusting to new distribution and display technologies. The chapters on radio and movies and the VCR deal with technologies that predate digitization technologies. As you will see, things were exciting then; however, it is after the advent of digitization and networked computers that things get really interesting.

THE NATURE OF INFORMATION

Information is agnostic about how it is expressed. All information conforms to certain economic dynamics that are dual-edged swords for the owners of information. The economic dynamics of information have been explored by economists since the 1970s. When considering the dynamics of content and technology today, it is important to understand a few main concepts of the economics of information.

Most of the headaches experienced by content owners stem from the fact that information is usually costly to produce initially but cheap to reproduce.[3] This has been true for most of the twentieth century, certainly before the age of the computer and the Internet, although these technologies make this rule even more important. Take as an example the costs involved in producing a record. It costs a lot to discover and record a singer. Often recording companies have to maintain armies of advance teams to frequent clubs around the world looking for talent. These expenses can be thought of as part of a record company's research and development (R&D) costs. Then there is considerable cost involved in recording the singer and marketing the resulting CD. In 2002, one major record label, MCA, spent $2.2 million to produce and market an album by a promising young singer named Carly Hennessy. The CD, *Ultimate High*, sold only 378 units for total revenues of only $4,900.[4] While this example was extreme enough to warrant the attention of the front page of the *Wall Street Journal*, it underscores a reality of any "hit business": there are more failures than winners.

However, after the album is produced and, with lots of luck, a star is born, the cost of printing every additional copy of the CD, the so-called marginal cost, is negligible. The same is true for most forms of information, such as software programs, movies, CDs, and books. The troublesome implication of this dynamic of information is that R&D and other costs associated with creating the first copy of content is often very steep, while the costs of piracy are usually quite cheap. The production cost of bootleg CDs is close to zero after the pirate copying factory has been paid for. And with digitized products, pirated copies can have the same quality as legitimate copies. That is not true of analog technologies, as evidenced by the many poor-quality copies of bootleg cassette tapes of, say, Pink Floyd, which may have proved irksome to the copyright holders but did not really damage sales of legitimate albums, tapes, and CDs.

When the popular filesharing services such as Napster emerged in 1999, which allowed users to trade online millions and millions of often perfect digitized music files, music companies became apoplectic, screaming that they were losing millions of dollars each year to pirates. To a large extent they were right. However, technology, in this case, the combination of digitized music, which has been around since the 1980s, and increasingly powerful and increasingly cheaper computers and the other essential ingredient, the network linking these computers provided by the Internet, combined to create a new market for music.

Unfortunately for the music companies, it created a market that they chose not to supply for a few years. The technologies that enabled filesharing to be so popular were not going away, even if the record companies were able to shut down Napster. Belatedly, the record industry hit upon a twin strategy: sue its potential customers and enter the new market themselves through proxies such as iTunes. Executed early enough, litigation, or better yet, an online distribution channel, might have kept Napster at bay. But the success of Napster (success measured by the millions of users it attracted; the company itself had not been profitable) meant that the filesharing genie was well out of its bottle by 1999. By the end of 2006, there still was no record-company-sanctioned filesharing service that had nearly the range of selection offered by Napster in 1999. Interestingly, the most successful legitimate online music store, iTunes, was created by a computer company looking to sell more computers as well as more iPods.

And filesharing is no longer just about trading music. Because music files are smaller than movie files (a four-minute song can be squeezed into many fewer zeros and ones than can a ninety-minute movie), digital distribution of movies had been slower to catch on. However, with larger bandwidth connections to the Internet becoming more common (think of bandwidth being like a soda straw—the fatter the straw, the easier it is to drink), Hollywood knows it will be next to be "Napsterized." This fear was tellingly expressed in October 2003 when the motion picture industry's main industry group and lobbyist, the powerful Motion Picture Association of America (MPAA), decided to ban the long-established practice of sending free videos and DVDs of movies to members of the Academy of Motion Picture Arts and Sciences, the folks whose votes equal coveted Oscars, due to fears about the risk of piracy, especially for movies that had not yet been released. Independent producers screamed because mailing videos and DVDs was the only way many of them had to reach academy members. In an eleventh-hour compromise, the MPAA decided to allow studios to send only DVDs watermarked to identify the recipient.

The twin forces of digitization and powerful PCs networked through the Internet raise the stakes for content owners, and the immensity of these stakes have doubtlessly influenced their decisions over the past few years. It is hard to blame the recording industry for being up in arms about piracy, but it is easy to find fault with their response. If the popularity of Napster proved anything it was that the recording industry fumbled a golden opportunity—and not just an opportunity to be robbed. The success of Apple Computer's iTunes service demonstrates the demand for legitimate, robust digital distribution of music. But the fear displayed by the recording industry, for example, in the face of new technological challenges and opportunities in the 1990s and into the 2000s is not a phenomenon that began with the advent of digital distribution. It reaches back to the beginning of the last century and that era's high tech.

OVERVIEW OF THE BUMPY ROAD TO PROSPERITY

For the past one hundred years, information industries exhibited a predictable reaction to technological change:

The Bumpy Road to Prosperity

1. Innovation: A new technology is born.

2. Ascension: The new technology takes root and grows into an industry.

3. Fear: The industry fears and resists technology changes that have an impact on their established models.

4. Prosperity: Innovation creates new markets and channels for existing industries.

This is ironic, not least because these industries began as technological innovations that in turn displaced something before them. This pattern can be seen in the early twentieth century, when music copyright owners resisted the evolution from selling their property via sheet music to the new channels created by player pianos, phonographs, and, later still, radio. The same pattern emerged in other information industries, including movies, television, and back to the again beleaguered music copyright owners.

Each of these industries underwent turmoil while going through the "Bumpy Road to Prosperity," forsaking new channels and markets while they resisted the change, but usually profiting in the end. Why? Mainly because the new technologies were quite apart from the existing technologies and businesses that occupied the established industries. Often the new channels failed to pay for the use of the property until revenue-sharing mechanisms were developed. The existing industries usually did not understand the new technology and initially failed to see how the change could benefit them.

Today, the confluence of separate but related forces—digitization, networking, and broadband—can create new avenues for information companies. In the past, the technological change was slow enough and limited enough that industries had the time to go through the pattern and emerge, at the end, in better shape than when they started. The forces at work today are too powerful to allow content companies that luxury. Now, unless information owners learn to break the pattern that has governed the way they look at new technologies, and instead work proactively to understand the impact (positive and negative) of the technology, they risk being swallowed by it.

The histories of radio, recorded music, movies, and television all show how new technologies that promised to spell a boon for established companies or industries were badly fumbled or outright opposed by those companies or groups that stood to gain the most. Sometimes the problem was a failure to exercise enlightened self-interest with one's property—in the cases discussed here that property is usually protected by copyright. In the 1930s, as radio was into its so-called "Golden Age," the country's only performing rights agency, the American Society of Composers, Authors and Publishers (ASCAP), doubled and then doubled again the rates it charged radio stations to play its copyrighted music. Radio essentially was the only means for introducing new music to the public, aside from motion pictures, which ASCAP subsequently alienated, and jukeboxes, which carried relatively few new tunes. For its efforts, ASCAP opened the door to new competition, after a twenty-five-year monopoly, and also drew the attention of the antitrust division of the Justice Department. Fumbling on an even larger scale by music copyright holders would be repeated by the music industry at the end of the twentieth century as it grappled to deal with another innovative medium, the Internet, even more sweeping in its potential to help exploit copyrights than had been seen with radio.

New technologies almost always initially seem to compete with existing ways of doing business (in a phrase, business models). Incumbents often fail to see new possibilities offered by new technologies because they are worried about the immediate impact on their established business models. Such was the case with movie studios in the late 1940s and their opposition to broadcast television. However, television turned into a gold mine for movie studios, providing an outlet for the studios' libraries of films and a new customer for their production facilities. Soon, television-related income accounted for 60 percent of studio revenue.[5]

In turn, broadcast television and the movie studios ganged up to oppose the videocassette recorder. Beginning in 1976, movie studios tried to ban the nascent home video recording industry. Fearful of the impact that VCRs could have on the studios' ability to control their content, a group of movie and television studios, led by Universal Studios, sued the Sony Corporation, maker of the Betamax video recorder. An appeals court found in favor of the studios, and the case went to the Supreme Court. The Supreme Court, in a 5 to 4 decision, narrowly reversed the appeals court ruling and found that the ability of VCRs to record broadcast television for private viewing at a more convenient time represented a legitimate use for the technology.

In the end, radio proved to be an important complement to recorded music, television proved to be a cash machine for movie studios, and as for that evil device, the VCR, around 60 percent of the annual revenue of major studios now comes from home video sales.

THE PLAN OF THIS BOOK

In considering the intersection of entertainment and technology, it is helpful to look at how our selected industries got to where they are today. This is not just because these stories are interesting but because often the seeds of our behavior are sown in our past formative experiences. This is true for individuals and it is true for industries, which after all are just collections of individuals. Each of the four stages (Innovation, Ascension, Fear, and Prosperity) is discussed in its own respective chapter using examples of different technologies and content industries.

Chapter 2 looks at the Innovation stage and shows how radio, the recording industry, movies, and television came about and made it through this initial stage. We see how innovation can come from anywhere (from the individual genius to corporate programs) but how each must be given room to grow and must have a business model capable of pushing the technology into the next stage.

Chapter 3 examines the Ascension stage and shows the importance of factors such as "network effects," "lock-in," and complementarity (in other words, two things making each other better) on our technologies over the course of the past century, and how they can propel a technology through the Ascension stage. We see how radio, records, movies, and television became big industries and how peer-to-peer technology may be poised for similar success. We also look at why some industries failed to graduate from the Ascension stage.

Chapter 4 looks at the Fear stage. The technological forces that drive so much progress today, especially in information industries, simultaneously affect different entrenched industries. This is why today the journey from the

Innovation to Fear stages and the resistance that goes with Fear is so quick. In the grip of the Fear stage, executives often see new complements only as competitors and fail to make the leap to envision new channels and businesses that can benefit them. This is why the recording industry spent so much energy shutting down Napster and so little energy trying to create a legal alternative. Fear is also the reason that the movie industry objected to television and tried to sue the VCR out of existence, even though both of these technologies ended up making the movie industry tons of money. For established industries in the Fear mode, their weapon of choice is usually copyright law, so we also look at the recent changes in legislation concerning intellectual property and explore how IP laws can play a more positive role for consumers and content industries.

Chapter 5 looks at the Prosperity stage. To get to Prosperity, movie studios had to think a little bit differently about their businesses and their relationships with customers. That usually is a prerequisite for incumbent industries to enter the Prosperity stage with a new technology. For example, both television and the VCR weakened the roles of movie theaters (exhibitors) in the long-established and cozy movie industry value chain. (The phrase *value chain* describes the steps taken to transform raw material into a product consumed by an end user. In the movie industry, the story idea might be the first link in the value chain and exhibitors and home viewers the final link.) Movie studios had to accommodate new value chains that these technologies thrust upon them.

Chapter 6 looks at how today's technologies have the ability to focus or atomize (choose your word) the traditional value proposition offered by content companies and provides lessons that executives and other stakeholders can learn to propel their companies into or stay in the Prosperity stage. I discuss specific steps that executives should take and that shareholders and other stakeholders should look for in companies that seek to operate at the intersection of entertainment and technology, and offer five rules for success for content companies and technology companies in a converged world.

The two appendices take a closer look at the technological forces that will drive today's convergence of content and technology and offer a brief background of important elements of IP protection. If you have ever uttered the phrase *Moore's Law* or would like a little more information on important IP concepts, it will be worth your time to dip into the appendices.

WHY TODAY'S THREATS AND
OPPORTUNITIES ARE SO PROFOUND

In the past, the information industries had time to, paraphrasing Winston Churchill, do the right thing after they exhausted all the other options. The new forces, however, are fundamentally different from the forces that information companies feared but ultimately benefited from in the past.

Technology changed this. Consumers already had digitized music at their fingertips, thanks to the millions of CDs that turned the languishing back catalogs of record companies into gold mines in the 1980s and 1990s. But, mix CDs with computers networked to the Internet, and stir in software that can copy a CD and convert its songs into a compressed MP3 file, and—this is another very important ingredient—absent any fundamental change in business model, you have a poisonous brew for record companies. If any lesson can be drawn from "the Noble Experiment" of Prohibition in the 1920s and 1930s, it is this: without a legal way to do it, people still will drink. In this case, people download music (fileshare), because they can and because it is a terrific way to consume content. Even a twelve-year-old honor student living in public housing and a seventy-one-year old grandmother, both targets of the Recording Industry Association of America (RIAA) (the trade lobby that represents the world's largest record companies) lawyers in a legal action really did—illegally—download over a thousand songs each. And it's not just the beleaguered record industry that is losing sleep. They may be canaries in coal mines for their bigger cousins. Movie studios feel, with justification, that they are next to be affected by the forces that roiled record companies. In addition to the MPAA's action described earlier, witness the ads that run during movie previews featuring hardworking movie crew members, ordinary folks, not the high-flying stars, directors, and producers, telling you how piracy will hurt their livelihood. They are right of course, but they are spitting in the wind.

This wind, more of a typhoon really, has picked up speed in the past ten years. PC functionality in terms of speed, memory, graphics, and display technology grew rapidly through the 1990s. Technology advances combined with cheaper broadband access, innovations in consumer electronics devices, and improved Internet interactivity during this period enabled the desktop PC to become a powerful multimedia tool. Amidst this technology and Internet development, entertainment emerged as one of the most popular categories on the Internet—after search engines and portals, entertainment domains were more in demand than both "news" and "information" as well as finance and investment-related Websites.

The ability of digitized content (in the form of the PC) to move out of the home office and into the living room—along the way breaking down established value chains and ways of creating, distributing, and getting paid for content—has been much talked about, although little has happened until now. As is being played out in the headlines today, television studios are grappling with threats and opportunities represented by upstart Internet companies such as YouTube. Seemingly overnight this former garage startup has attracted millions of viewers to videos posted on its site. Some of this content was copyrighted segments of broadcast television shows: for example, a funny sketch from NBC's *Saturday Night Live*. Some SNL segments recorded from the televised broadcast and posted by users on YouTube reached many millions more viewers than SNL ever did even in its heyday. At first, NBC made YouTube remove the videos because they infringed on NBC's copyright. But within months, the network did an about face and announced an advertising deal with the site. It was catching on to the requirement for Prosperity; it was thinking differently about itself and its business.

The surest ticket to the Prosperity stage has always been to give consumers new and profitable ways to enjoy content. This is often what new technologies do. However, as we have seen in the past it has not always been immediately clear to content owners how they would prosper from the new technologies. Technology companies either because they were too nascent to have clout or disinterested did not compel content owners to come along. Content owners usually lacked sufficient insight into new technologies (regrettable but understandable) and sufficient imagination (far less forgivable) until somebody showed them the way to Prosperity. Even having content and technology exist within the same company does not guarantee success. In these cases, the technology and content sides of the business do not seem to communicate with each other and might as well be separate.

CONCLUSION

This book looks broadly at examples within the entertainment industry of the twentieth century and into the twenty-first century. This is not to pick on one industry or even American entertainment moguls, who by and large make products that are in demand all over the world. Rather, because their products are so successful and so familiar to us all, the foibles and failures of these content owners affect us all, and not just in how we consume their products.

The ability to fashion successful new business models for distributing and consuming information has powerful knock-on effects for important complementary industries such as telecommunications and computing. The salutary effects of wider penetration of consumer broadband, and in turn the dependence of higher broadband penetration upon the wider availability of digital content, has been described by many researchers.

A better marriage of technology and content will have powerful benefits for consumers and shareholders of companies that produce the content and the technology used to consume it. Many economists point to networking as the crucial link between increased IT performance and productivity gains. Networks, essentially any connection between two or more computers, are made far more robust by broadband.

Broadband is an important potential catalyst for general economic growth in the United States. A Brookings Institution study conducted in July 2001 estimated that broadband could add $500 billion per year to the United States economy.[6] The study found that consumers would benefit from enhanced online home shopping and entertainment services as well as from a variety of additional services. The researchers estimated that $400 billion per year could be derived from such services while an additional $50 billion to $100 billion per year could be added to the economy from broadband-related gains experienced by manufacturers of computers, software, and entertainment products.

Indeed, e-commerce annual revenue in the United States grew from nothing in the early 1990s to around $12 billion in 2001 and exceeded $80 billion in 2005.[7] A May 1999 survey by Mercer Management Consulting in Washington, D.C., showed that people with high-speed access search for information and make purchases online at approximately double the rate of those who access the Internet with a dial-up connection.[8] According to the Pew Internet and American Life Project, by 2005, 53 percent of home Internet users had broadband.[9] However, the rate of broadband adoption was actually slowing in the United States due to the high cost of broadband service and a lack of content on the Internet compelling enough to entice dial-up Internet users.

For the millions who socialize online via MySpace, watch videos on YouTube, shop at Amazon, and make their phone calls over the Internet, there are many, many more who do none of these things and will not until there is more compelling content online. Fear prevents executives from making the leap to prosperity. Consumers lose out, and so do shareholders.

2 INNOVATION

A S ANY TEXT MESSAGER CAN TELL YOU, the letters *CQ* stand for "seek you" and invite response. It was the same one hundred years ago with the text message technology of that day, Morse code, when an inventor built on several innovations and changed the world. On Christmas Eve in 1906 from a lab on the Massachusetts coast radio pioneer Reginald Fessenden tapped out "CQ, CQ" over airwaves that until this moment had carried only electric pulses of dots and dashes. Anybody listening to this particular transmission was soon to be astonished. What followed was not more dots and dashes conveying information on ship arrivals or a news item; it was a voice! Nobody had ever heard a voice over radio before, and stunned operators called everybody within earshot to listen. The voice was a recording of a woman singing a Handel aria followed by an amateur violin solo (by Fessenden himself). The broadcast was heard by radio operators far and wide, including a few on banana boats in the West Indies.[1]

Innovation takes many forms. Sometimes it seems as random as a lightning strike, other times it feels predictable, like flowers blooming on schedule in a hothouse. Innovations may vary in how they are conceived, but the pathway that runs from innovation to changing the world and maybe making a pile of money usually follows the four common waypoints or stages described in Chapter 1. In this chapter, we start with the first stage: Innovation.

It is important to understand the dynamics of innovation because the ability of executives and regulators to think clearly about the Innovation stage, learn from the past, and navigate their way forward has an impact on share-holders, employees, and consumers. The technologies discussed in this book include the lightning strikes, albeit hitting well-prepared inventors, and the hothouse variety, for example the serial innovations emerging from Thomas Edison's development labs.

The great entertainment technologies of the twentieth century—radio, recording, movies, television, and filesharing—were discrete innovations. That does not mean that they came to us fully formed from individual geniuses. As you will read, they did not. Nor does it mean that the innovation that created these technologies wasn't messy; it was. However, these technologies were discrete in that they did not bump up against their competitors (and possible successors) until they were somewhat established.

Much innovation today does not have this luxury. The technological forces that drive so much progress today, especially in information industries, simultaneously affect different entrenched industries. This is why today the journey from Innovation to Fear and the resistance that goes with fear is so quick. In this chapter we look at how some technologies in the past entered and navigated the Innovation stage. Although the technologies and stories differ, there are some common traits that are important to understand when one thinks about how a technology makes it through this stage. A closer look at how radio, the recording industry, motion pictures, television, and filesharing came about shows how messy innovation usually is.

SURFING THE HERTZIAN WAVE: THE EARLY HISTORY OF RADIO

At the beginning of the twentieth century—when radio waves carried only dots and dashes—one visionary described the new wireless technology as bringing a day when "families and friends each have [their] own wireless system with its own secret tune."[2] However, this would not come to pass for over twenty years. In the first years of the twentieth century, radio was dominated by the Marconi Company, founded in 1897 by Guglielmo Marconi, a twenty-three year old amateur inventor who would become known as the "Father of Radio."

The young Guglielmo was a slight and studious child. He was educated at private schools in England and Italy. In his teens, Guglielmo developed an interest in physics and electricity. Benjamin Franklin was a special hero to him, and like Franklin, Marconi became an avid amateur experimenter, setting up a laboratory in his parent's attic.[3] It was a propitious time for advances in the technology that would become radio. The work of the British physicist James Clerk Maxwell in the 1860s had established the theory of radio waves. The German physicist Heinrich Hertz in the 1880s succeeded in producing and detecting the waves described by Maxwell. These and other discoveries underpinned the technology for wireless transmission of signals.

In 1894, while on a family summer vacation in the Italian Alps, Marconi came across an article on Hertzian waves. Marconi became convinced that these waves could be used for communication. He cut short his vacation and returned to his family's villa to work in his attic laboratory.

Marconi was only one of many researchers experimenting with the equipment that was available at that time. After a little research and practice, Marconi was able to achieve results similar to other experimenters, sending signals over a distance of a few yards. With thoughts of Benjamin Franklin's kite and lightning rod, Marconi even made a sidetrack, experimenting with techniques to detect electrical storms with tall antennas, but soon gave up this research and returned to his Hertzian wave experiments.[4]

It was at this time that Marconi hit upon the inspiration that set him apart from other researchers. Marconi combined the elevated antenna he used in his weather research with his apparatus and achieved a tremendous increase in the range he could send and detect a wave. He was achieving distances of one and a half miles compared to the maximum of perhaps one hundred yards achieved by other experimenters. With further improvements, Marconi was able to introduce a Morse code key into his apparatus and used it to send the dot-and-dash telegraphic signals over then-speechless radio waves.

An enthusiastic Marconi demonstrated his invention to the Italian government. They were uninterested. Dejected, Marconi took the advice of his maternal uncles (who were heir to the Jameson Irish whiskey fortune) and tried to interest the British government in the device. In February 1895, at the age of twenty-one, Marconi and his mother set sail for England. There they met a warmer reception. With a far-flung empire and a mighty navy dispersed to defend it, the British government was better disposed than the Italian government to receiving and promoting novel communication technologies.

In July 1897 the British government issued Marconi the world's first patent on radio technology. Later that month, at the age of twenty-three, Marconi and a group of British investors formed the Wireless Telegraph and Signal

Company, Ltd., later renamed Marconi's Wireless Telegraph Company, Ltd. The company was capitalized at £100,000 (equivalent to £7.35 million in 2004).[5] Marconi received half of the shares, £15,000 in cash, and became one of six directors of the startup.[6]

As early as 1897, Marconi speculated that his wireless telegraph would have military uses. Marconi also speculated darkly that his wave could be used to explode powder on ships, as Hertz had demonstrated using electric waves.[7] But the first uses of Marconi's invention would be peaceful. In many countries apart from the United States, particularly before the Thatcherite privatization movements of the 1970s and 1980s, most communications technologies, such as the post, telegraph, and telephone, came under the auspices of national governments. In Britain, laws prohibited Marconi from using his wireless technology to offer telegraph services in competition with the existing British Post Office's wired telegraph service.[8] Marconi had to look elsewhere for a market. Shipping communication seemed the most promising.

Initially, Marconi viewed the technology as a wireless telegraph ("wireless telegraphy"), and he set about to perfect this model of the technology. Marconi sought to perfect radio along the lines of telegraphy, increasing transmission speed (of the Morse code that it broadcast) and improving tuning to make the transmission more secure from incidental or intended eavesdropping.[9]

The young company moved to the south of England on the Isle of Wight and began experiments, transmitting signals to the coast, separated by fourteen miles of sea and often inclement weather. In December 1901 signals from a high-power Marconi transmitter located at Cornwall, England, were reported to have been picked up by a receiving station near St. John's in Newfoundland. The receiving antenna was a four-hundred-foot-long copper wire supported by a kite, and the detector was an Italian Navy coherer consisting of a globule of mercury between iron terminals and connected to a telephone receiver. In January 1903 a Marconi station at Cape Cod, Massachusetts, sent a short message from President Theodore Roosevelt to King Edward VII in England.

MARCONI (AND ONLY MARCONI) CALLING

Marconi set out to control the business of radio, as the company then envisaged it. He set up business practices that would have made Bill Gates blush. In particular, Marconi's company sought to establish noninterconnection with competing radio companies and then tried to claim that its services comprised a system which could not be disintermediated. (A similar claim would be used over ninety years later by Microsoft in its antitrust trial when it claimed that its Explorer Web browser was too thoroughly integrated into the Windows operating system to be disintermediated.)

Marconi built his business around company-owned listening stations that picked up signals broadcast by Marconi-employed operators tapping out messages on Marconi-owned radio sets that had been leased to ships. The first major market for Marconi was naval and commercial shipping communications. By 1900, Marconi had interested the U.S. Navy in the technology. Other Navies too were interested, and Marconi supplied both the British Royal Navy and the Italian Navy with wireless sets.

In 1901, a newspaper, the *New York Herald,* hired Marconi to gain advance reports from ships, including information on their arrivals to U.S. ports through wireless communications with a Marconi land station in Nantucket.

Marconi's biggest contract was with famed insurer Lloyd's of London. In 1901, Marconi signed a contract to lease Marconi wireless sets to ships insured by Lloyds. These sets were run by Marconi-employed operators who communicated only with Marconi land stations. Under the terms of the contract, Marconi established its nonintercommunication policy: the company would neither transmit nor receive messages produced by other companies. At the time, Lloyds was by far the largest marine insurer in the world and most goods were shipped by sea. Marconi's nonintercommunication policy forced shippers who did business with Lloyds, or hoped to do business with Lloyds, to use Marconi services. This was an example of an attempt to capture network effects associated with technologies.

With the Lloyds contract in his pocket, Marconi built out the company's infrastructure, adding to its chain of shore stations. In early 1902, Marconi said that he expected to spend less than $150,000 (a little over $3.2 million in 2003) to build and equip land stations on both sides of the Atlantic. Maintenance costs were low. Marconi operators could transmit about twenty words a minute. In 1902, Marconi charged about twelve cents per word (equivalent to $2.56 in 2003) for transmission across the Atlantic. By comparison, a telegraph cable across the Atlantic cost between $3 million and $4 million to install and required constant costly upkeep.[10] In 1902, some estimated that about $400,000,000 (equivalent to $8.55 billion in 2003) was invested in telegraph systems around the world.[11] This was a rich market for Marconi.

By 1899, Marconi had incorporated the Marconi Wireless Company of

America (American Marconi), capitalized at $10,000,000, in order to exploit his patents in the United States. Marconi maintained tight control of the company from London. This foreign ownership would cause the company problems in the future as wireless became more important to national security.

Unfortunately for Marconi, dots and dashes were pretty much the same, regardless of whether they were generated by Marconi sets or those of competitors. Rival equipment could communicate with Marconi's equipment. Indeed emergency messages were received and relayed as part of an agreement.

Marconi tried to establish a valuable brand by promoting Marconi equipment as more advanced than those operated by rivals. The company claimed that it did not want to risk damaging the reputation of the nascent wireless communications industry by interconnecting with inferior services.[12] Actually, the company relied on nonintercommunication to defend its interests because it lacked the financial resources to protect them in court.[13] In a 1904 letter discussing the company's position in an infringement suit against another radio pioneer, Lee de Forest (see next section), Marconi managing director H. Cuthbert Hall wrote, "I would rather not fight. We have nothing to gain commercially or in prestige by a win, and we should lose a little in prestige if we lost. . . . Our position now depends far more on contracts than on patents. . . ."[14]

This position was taken out of necessity. Marconi did not have the money to fight many patent battles. The Marconi Company did not show a profit until 1911 because the company reinvested much of its cash flow into expansion. In addition, revenue from wireless shipboard traffic did not turn out to add up to as much as Marconi had planned. Unfortunately for the Marconi Company, much of the early ship-to-shore wireless traffic consisted of good wishes sent by first-class passengers in the hours after setting out and before returning. Passengers had little appetite for sending and receiving "Marconis" over the weeks of a typical voyage.[15]

Marconi's failure to embrace voice over the radio and modify his business model beyond "Marconigrams" prevented his company from transcending the Innovation stage.

VOICES IN THE AIR

Other pioneers, fast on the heels of Marconi, brought a different vision to radio technology. Three in particular would shape radio as we know it today: Reginald A. Fessenden, a former employee of Thomas Edison and later Westinghouse, and later still a university professor; Lee de Forest, a researcher with Western Electric, the equipment maker for AT&T, who experimented with wireless communication in his spare time; and Edwin H. Armstrong, an independent researcher at Columbia University. Each of these experimenters had deep entrepreneurial streaks and a vision that the goal of wireless technology should be the transmission not just of dots and dashes, but rich sounds such as music and voice. To do this, it was necessary to move beyond Marconi's use of intermittent, highly damped waves and create an apparatus that would transmit and receive continuous waves.[16] Between 1899 and 1902, Marconi, Fessenden, and de Forest each formed his own wireless company in the United States.

In 1900, Fessenden left his college teaching job and accepted an offer by the U.S. Weather Bureau to test a plan to disseminate weather information via wireless. While working for the Weather Bureau, he was thinking about creating a wireless transmission system, not for sending Morse code but for voice communication. Sending voice over a radio wave marked a major change in thinking about the technology. Fessenden proposed using a continuous wave to carry a voice as variations or modulations instead of an interrupted wave, as was used by Marconi. This became the foundation of radio as we know it. By 1902, Fessenden had succeeded in using a telephone microphone to add a voice to a radio wave.

Radio voice transmission far exceeded the interests and funding of the Weather Bureau. Also, Fessenden worried about the government gaining ownership of his work should he continue in the employ of the Weather Bureau. In 1902, Fessenden managed to interest two Pittsburgh financiers, T. H. Given and Hay Walker Jr., in his work. The three men founded a company, the National Electric Signaling Company (NESCO), with the financiers contributing $1,000,000 (equivalent to over $21.3 million in 2003) and Fessenden contributing his patents and sweat.

By late 1906, NESCO's system was ready for a test. In the Christmas Eve broadcast described earlier, Fessenden became the world's first DJ.

But this broadcast was about as far as NESCO got. The United Fruit Company purchased some of NESCO's equipment in order to communicate with ships and direct their perishable cargoes to the ports offering the highest prices. (This was a commercial application of the broad idea that the Weather Service had wanted when they had contacted Fessenden in 1900.) But like weekend golfers on the tee, people were more impressed by distance than by quality; the public's attention was more attracted by Marconi and his crossing of the Atlantic with Morse code on intermittent waves than by voice transmissions on continuous waves, which some viewed as an unnecessary frill.[17] In 1911, Fessenden fell out with his backers and left NESCO. The company went into receivership. Later Fessenden became embroiled in a protracted patent dispute with Radio Corporation of America (RCA), which was eventually settled out of court. The proceeds allowed him to retire to Bermuda.

Soon after Fessenden's broadcast debut, another radio pioneer, Lee de Forest, took to the air. In March 1907, de Forest played phonograph records over the air, broadcasting from the top floor of the Parker Building in Manhattan. Soon he invited singers to his laboratory. The first, a Miss van Boos, sang "I Love You Truly," and was heard by radio operators in the Brooklyn Ship Yard. Around this time, de Forest would make many solid contributions to radio, including being the first to conceive of the broadcast model, but he would also become entangled in one of the technology's first stock manipulations and frauds.

Graduating Yale in 1899 with a Ph.D., de Forest found his first job with Western Electric, the manufacturing arm of American Telephone and Telegraph (AT&T). The job suited de Forest, who was interested in voice transmission and whose one indulgence was an occasional visit to the opera. In an entry in his diary at this time de Forest wrote, "What finer task than to transfer the sound of a voice of song to one a thousand miles away. If I could do that tonight!"[18] In his spare time, de Forest experimented with radio. In a lab set up in his rented room, de Forest reproduced the experiments of Marconi and others. He soon had an improved radio apparatus.

In 1901, emboldened by his success, de Forest set out to test his apparatus at the America's Cup yacht races off Sandy Hook, New York. De Forest received $1,000 from a newswire service to report the results of the race. It would be a crowded test of the new technology. Marconi himself had been hired by the *New York Herald* to perform the same service, and a third, unaffiliated radio researcher was also there to show off his apparatus. With three transmitters vying for the same airwaves, the radio systems produced more cacophony than intelligible signal. It was a complete fiasco. However, the newspaper and wire service, which had promoted their wireless coverage of the races, took the precaution of also obtaining results by semaphore. They did not reveal that the radio coverage had been a bust; instead de Forest found himself lauded for this (imagined) feat of new technology alongside the world-famous Marconi.

The press coverage brought de Forest to the attention of a financier and promoter named Abraham White, whom de Forest described as "a very personable Wall Street character." In 1902, the two men incorporated the De Forest Wireless Telegraph Company, capitalized at $3,000,000 (equivalent to over $85.4 million in 2003). De Forest received a block of stock and a salary of $20 per week, and continued with his experiments. However, unlike Fessenden's backers, who kept their company private, White immediately set out to issue public shares in the company.

De Forest and White began drumming up interest in the company. De Forest gave demonstrations in major cities and even displayed himself working with his apparatus in a glass house at the 1904 St. Louis World's Fair. The public snapped up the company's shares, and White recapitalized the company to $15,000,000 (equivalent to over $308 million in 2003).

The next year de Forest developed a new wireless detector he called the "grid audion." This device was an important element in making radio viable as an industry. De Forest later said of his audion, "Unwittingly then, had I discovered an Invisible Empire of the Air."[19]

In 1907 de Forest received a patent for the audion and along with three other partners established a new company, the De Forest Radio Telephone Company, to exploit his invention. De Forest did not have in mind wireless telephony as we think of cell phones today, but rather broadcast radio. He played records over the air and had singers perform. In 1908, using his grid audion, de Forest broadcast from the Eiffel Tower while on his honeymoon in Paris. The broadcast was picked up as far as five hundred miles away.

Meanwhile, de Forest's first company was being pulled out from under him in sharp practice by White. The financier and some of his cronies had formed a new company, United Wireless Telegraph Company, capitalized at $20,000,000 (equivalent to over $389 million in 2003) and assumed control of the De Forest Wireless Telegraph Company. The transaction left nothing of value to the original shareholders, including De Forest.

At about the time that Reginald Fessenden was washing his hands of NESCO, de Forest was facing severe financial straits. The De Forest Radio Telephone Company had suffered a rough six years. Its successes, including the twenty-six sets sold to the U.S. Navy, which they used on their "Great White Fleet" around-the-world tour in 1907, were exceeded by the promises of de Forest and his company's executives. By 1907, much of the easy capital that had been available to radio startups had become harder to find. One business magazine of the time described it as a "Wireless Telegraph Bubble" and ran pictures of White and de Forest above a cartoon of Hertzian waves pulling money out of investor's pockets.[20] In this bear market for radio, de Forest and his directors were careful to pay small dividends from the beginning, gaining investor confidence. They then set up subsidiary companies, such as the Atlantic Radio Telephone Company and the Great Lakes Radio Company. Both companies were capitalized at $2.5 million each.

The De Forest Radio Telephone Company promised to build broadcast stations around the country, but in the end only eleven were built and they worked only fitfully. Although his business practices were not absolutely aboveboard, de Forest was the first to anticipate the broadcast future of wireless technology. He told the *New York Times* in 1909, "I look forward to the day when opera may be brought into every home. Someday the news and even advertising will be sent out over the wireless telephone."[21] For all of his predictions, the company had very little success.

By 1912, investors had had enough with promises. They sought action against de Forest and the other founders. The trial that ensued revealed that of the $1,597,505 earned from sales of stock, only $345,694 actually made it to the companies. The remainder went to its founders. The trial also revealed that an exhibition of long-distance radio telephony between Paris, France, and Great Lake Company office, and subsequently relayed to the office of the newspaper the *Milwaukee Journal,* had been faked. The transmission had come from a telegraph station four blocks from the newspaper.[22] At 1 A.M. on New Year's Day in 1914 the jury returned its verdict: two of the partners were found guilty; de Forest and another were found innocent.

Not surprisingly, de Forest was again nearly broke by this time. His one asset was his grid audion patent. In October 1912, de Forest had demonstrated his audion as a telephone line amplifier for AT&T, the phone company. It worked very well. Perhaps sensing his desperation, however, the telephone company left de Forest twisting in the wind. The company did not follow up quickly or directly. As told by the late historian Erik Barnouw in *A Tower in Babel,* relating what de Forest wrote in his autobiography (a work not considered by historians to be completely reliable), de Forest was approached in the summer of 1913 by an attorney seeking to purchase rights to the audion. The attorney gave his "word of honor as a gentleman" that he did not represent AT&T, but also could not reveal his client. The attorney offered de Forest $50,000 (equivalent to over $900,000 in 2003) for the rights to the audion. De Forest, nearly broke, accepted. De Forest wrote that he later learned that the attorney had indeed represented AT&T, and the company would have been willing to pay up to half a million dollars for the rights. Still, de Forest later sold additional rights to AT&T for $90,000 and later still sold all of his remaining patents to the company for $250,000. De Forest retained the right to sell his equipment to the amateur market.[23]

It was at this time that patent wars concerning the technology began heating up. In 1916, the United States District Court in New York City found that the de Forest grid audion infringed on the original audion, the patent for which was owned by the Marconi Company. Thus de Forest's grid audion could not be marketed in the United States without the consent of the Marconi Company. However, the court also ruled that the electrode grid that de Forest had added to the audion was protected by de Forest's patent. This was a financially empty victory for de Forest since he had already sold the rights to the grid to AT&T.[24]

De Forest has often been described as both a charlatan and a genius. His contribution to radio is certainly mixed. For example, he did not completely understand why his grid audion worked. A talented Columbia University undergraduate named Edwin H. Armstrong, who researched it, did understand. Armstrong had devised a way to use a feedback circuit, the so-called "regenerative circuit," to return current through the audion to reinforce itself. This feedback circuit, for which Armstrong received a patent in 1914, allowed the audion to generate radio waves as well as detect them. It became a key milestone in the commercialization of radio.

VOICES CARRY: THE EARLY HISTORY OF THE RECORDING INDUSTRY

Like so much else, the recording industry began with Thomas Edison. The inventor had been working to develop a method of recording and retransmitting messages over the telegraph and telephone when he hit on the idea of constructing a device for recording sound. According to early-recording authority Allen Koenigsberg, others experimented with the essential concept of recording sound before Edison. Koenigsberg cites the example in 1806 of the English physician and naturalist Thomas Young, who registered vibrations of a tuning fork on a rotating drum covered with wax. The purpose was to use an established frequency to measure very small units of time. Koenigsberg also mentions that in 1859 a French librarian and typesetter named Leon

Scott improved Young's device in order to record voice as well as sound traces. This device later became known as the "vibrograph." Scott sold a few of his devices, which he called the "phonautograph," one of which ended up in the Smithsonian Institution in 1866. Koenigsberg tantalizes with the unverified story that Scott had visited the White House and made a recording of Abraham Lincoln, who as an inventor and patent holder himself would have been intrigued with the device.[25]

Edison was not looking to record voices when he developed his phonograph. In 1877, Edison was trying to develop a machine that would transcribe telegraphic messages through indentations on paper tape. The goal was to use the "tape recordings" to repeatedly send the same message over telegraphs. However, Edison also made a leap and speculated that a telephone message could also be recorded in a similar fashion. (The world's first answering machine?) He experimented with a diaphragm connected to a needle held against a rapidly moving paraffin-coated paper cylinder. The vibrations produced by speaking onto the diaphragm pushed the needle into the cylinder and made indentations in the paraffin-coated paper. According to Edison, he tested his "graphophone" by speaking into it and recording the nursery rhyme "Mary had a little lamb whose fleece was white as snow, and everywhere that Mary went the lamb was sure to go." Edison later changed to a metal cylinder with tin foil wrapped around it. The machine had two diaphragm-and-needle units, one for recording, and one for playback.

Ever thinking about marketing and how to transcend the Innovation stage, in January 1878 the inventor established the Edison Speaking Phonograph Company. Edison himself received $10,000 (equivalent to over $183,000 in 2003) for the manufacturing and sales rights and 20 percent of the profits. The machine sold well as a novelty, but that soon wore off and sales stalled.

Sidebar: Edison's Suggested Uses for the Phonograph

To break into larger markets, Edison suggested the following uses for his phonograph in an article in the *North American Review* in May 1878:[26]

- Letter writing and all kinds of dictation without the aid of a stenographer
- Phonographic books, which will speak to blind people without effort on their part

- The teaching of elocution
- Reproduction of music
- The "Family Record"—a registry of sayings, reminiscences, and so on, by members of a family in their own voices, and of the last words of dying persons
- Music boxes and toys
- Clocks that should announce in articulate speech the time for going home, going to meals, and so on
- The preservation of languages by exact reproduction of the manner of pronouncing
- Educational purposes, such as preserving the explanations made by a teacher, so that the pupil can refer to them at any moment
- Connection with the telephone, so as to make that instrument an auxiliary in the transmission of permanent and invaluable records, instead of being the recipient of momentary and fleeting communication

---

Eventually Edison turned his attention to inventing the incandescent light bulb. Still, over time, he made improvements to his phonograph and launched a new company, the Edison Phonograph Company, on October 8, 1887, to sell his improved phonograph.

Edison even used his phonograph technology to give voice to talking dolls. The Edison Phonograph Toy Manufacturing Company started production in 1890. The dolls contained tiny wax cylinders that played on a wind-up phonograph about seven inches tall that was placed within the body of the doll. The doll sold for $10 (equivalent to over $200 in 2003). Sales were poor, and Edison ended his relationship with the company in the following year. Another Edison company produced musical cylinders for coin-slot phonographs, which some of the subsidiary companies had started to use. These proto-"jukeboxes" were a development that pointed to the future of phonographs as entertainment machines. Initially, these machines were rented, but soon Edison changed to an outright sales model.

In 1894, the North American Phonograph Company (the company that had purchased early rights to the phonograph) declared bankruptcy. Edison, its majority shareholder, bought back the rights to his invention. It took two years for the bankruptcy affairs to be settled before Edison could move ahead with marketing his phonograph. The Edison Spring Motor Phonograph appeared in 1895, even though technically Edison was not allowed to sell phonographs at this time because of the bankruptcy agreement. By 1898, Edison was selling consumer versions of the phonograph called the Edison Standard Phonograph. Prices for the phonographs had dropped significantly from the technology's early days of $150 (over $3,000 in 2003) in 1891 down to $20 for the Standard model and $7.50 ($165 in 2003) for a model known as the Gem, introduced in 1899. Record cylinders, typically featuring marches, ballads, hymns, and comic monologues, sold for 50 cents ($11 in 2003).[27]

The early cylinder recordings ran for only two minutes, which constrained the content that could be recorded. Also, the cylinders were difficult to mass produce. A process for mass producing duplicate wax cylinders was put into effect in 1901. The cylinders were molded, rather than engraved by a stylus, and a harder wax was used.

Meanwhile, apart from Edison, other entrepreneurs were experimenting with the technology. In 1888 a German-born immigrant named Emile Berliner patented his device for etching sound onto a flat metal disc. Berliner's disc reproduced sound better than a cylinder, recorded up to four minutes of sound compared with two minutes available on cylinders, and was considerably easier to manufacture. Berliner also invented a new device with a turntable to play the discs, a machine he called a gramophone.

While it was an advance from its competition, the gramophone was not a commercial success. It was manually operated, so the speed of the turntable, and hence the quality of the sound given from the disc, depended upon the skill of the person turning the crank. In 1896, an engineer named Eldridge R. Johnson developed a spring motor that could rotate the turntable at a constant speed. Johnson went on to make improvements in the recording process as well.

Still, all was not happy for Berliner or Johnson. Berliner had appointed a company called the National Gramophone Company (NGA) as exclusive sales agent for the gramophone. Thus Berliner's and, since his invention was a component of Berliner's gramophone, Johnson's, fortunes were tied to NGA. This company produced and marketed its own machine, called the "zonophone," in preference to the Berliner device. Berliner and Johnson fell out with NGA and in September 1901 formed their own company called the Victor Talking Machine Company, with Johnson in control.[28]

LIGHTS, CAMERA, OLIGOPOLY:
HISTORY OF THE FILM INDUSTRY

Edison again. The legendary inventor introduced the world's first motion pictures at the Chicago World's Fair in 1893. Fairgoers paid to peer, one-by-one, into Edison's peephole Kinetoscope and view the short movie. With his Kinetoscope, Edison sought to reproduce the commercial success of his phonograph, which was then attracting patrons who paid a nickel to hear a brief recording through a set of earphones. In 1892 Edison and his colleague, William Kennedy Laurie Dickson, invented a camera they called the "Kinetograph" to record motion pictures and a peephole Kinetoscope for individualized viewing of the moving images filmed by the Kinetograph. In 1893 Edison built a motion picture studio near his New Jersey laboratory. After a series of delays, Edison completed the first twenty-five Kinetoscopes in January 1894. The devices were offered for sale in April of that year for $250 (equivalent to over $5,300 in 2003) per machine. The first Kinetoscope parlor opened in New York City in April 1894, and many others followed in cities across the country. Edison held patents on both the Kinetograph and Kinetoscope. Edison's profits from the sale of Kinetoscopes alone totaled $75,000 by March 1895. Competitors soon entered the market with their own versions of the Kinetoscope. From the beginning of the industry, Edison was more concerned with the revenue opportunities associated with the equipment used to record and display motion pictures than potential income available from the exhibition of his films.

By 1895, enhancements to the Edison kinetoscope process—made by entrepreneurs then unaffiliated with Edison—had improved the resulting image and allowed for its projection. The shift from individualized viewing to projection for a group fundamentally changed the business: where once motion pictures could only be viewed by an individual peering into a peephole, now films could be viewed by a roomful of people. The owners of exhibition rights offered a complete exhibition service that included a selection of films, a projector, and a projectionist. Their customers were often the vaudeville theaters that existed in cities across the country. These outlets provided the principal venues for motion pictures over the next ten years.

With the rise in popularity of movies came the nickelodeon, or "Nickel Theaters," in which features were shown regularly and titles changed frequently. Nickelodeons were located in large urban centers and initially offered programs between two and ten minutes in length. By 1906, nickelodeons were the industry's dominant exhibition outlets. As the industry grew, competitors entered, and the early patent holders such as Edison had mixed success defending their patents from challengers. In December 1908, the largest motion picture patent holders, Edison, The American Mustoscope and Biograph Company, and Vitagraph, formed the Motion Picture Patents Company (MPPC, referred to at the time as the motion pictures "Trust") to cooperatively license their patents and effectively control the nascent motion picture industry in the United States. In October 1915, the U.S. courts deemed MPPC an unlawful monopoly and ordered it to be dissolved.

THERE'S SOMETHING ON:
HISTORY OF THE TELEVISION INDUSTRY

To language purists, it is very bad form to mix Greek and Latin cognates when forming new words. Alas, that is exactly what *television* does. The redoubtable C. P. Scott, for almost sixty years editor of one of Britain's premier newspapers, *The Manchester Guardian* (now called *The Guardian*), said, "Television? The word is half Greek, half Latin. No good can come of it."[29] For a brief time in the early twentieth century, it looked as if the television itself, if it ever came about, would be a similarly mixed device, a combination of electronics and moving, mechanical parts.

The idea of television had been in the air at least since the 1880s. There were rumors that Alexander Graham Bell, inventor of the telephone, was working on something called a "photophone" in 1880. Also in that year, the British science journal *Nature* ran a letter describing a proposal for a process called "Mosaic" that used small squares of selenium as conductors connected to wires and batteries to transmit visual images.[30] (Mosaic was also the name of the world's first Internet browser, the direct ancestor of the Netscape Navigator.)

These ideas did not come to fruition. However, by early 1884, a twenty-three-year old German engineer named Paul Nipkow had received a German patent for the Nipkow spinning disc. This disc consisted of a series of twenty-four holes spiraling inward from the outer rim of the disc. When rotated, one disc would provide the scanning necessary to break an image into constituent parts. This disc acted like a transmitter when placed such that it blocked light from the viewed object to a photosensitive transmitter (a photocell). Then the disc was rotated, the first hole would sweep across the picture, then the next hole, and so on. One revolution of the disc would give one complete scan. The photocell transmitted to another disc acting as the receiver. This disc was set up in reverse of the transmitter. When the receiving cell received a current of electricity, it would light a bulb. If it did not receive the current, the bulb would remain dark. If the entire scan took less than one-tenth of a second, the human eye would see the result as one complete picture. If the object were moving, the disc would show it again, but a moment later, as it had moved. Successive revolutions would produce successive pictures of, for example, a man walking across a room.[31]

Nipkow did not advance his device beyond his patent. However, the spinning disc had been the common denominator of most subsequent tries at developing a television technology. By the 1920s inventors such as the Scotsman John Logie Baird and the American Charles Francis Jenkins were able to develop electromechanical television systems that used a variation of the Nipkow disc, and began rudimentary broadcasts. The fatal flaw of any electromechanical television system, however, lay with the "mechanical" part: the spinning disc. The spinning disc could never produce a good image because it could not spin fast enough to avoid flicker, nor could holes be cut small enough or close together enough to give good resolution.[32] An all-electrical system would be necessary if television was to develop into a robust medium. Such a system was being conceived—by a teenager in rural Idaho.

Philo T. Farnsworth was fifteen years old when in 1922 he conceived of the idea of an all-electrical television system. Farnsworth was precocious like the young Marconi, but where Marconi had come from wealth, Farnsworth had a far more hardscrabble background. His grandparents were Mormons who had walked thirteen hundred miles to Utah with Brigham Young. Farnsworth had been born in Utah but his family moved to a ranch in Rigby, Idaho, when he was fourteen. As a young child, Philo, who was called Phil by his family, was deeply interested in science and invention. His parents indulged his interests by subscribing to the popular science magazines of the day, stoking in Farnsworth the zeitgeist for science combined with practical invention that seems to have caught Fessenden, de Forest, and Armstrong, although they were older than Phil when they took up inventing.

Farnsworth first sketched the rough idea for an all-electrical television system on a chalkboard during his freshman year of high school. He continued thinking about and experimenting with the idea as he entered college.

To help support his family while in college, Farnsworth tried his hand at a variety of jobs, working as a school janitor during the year and in a lumber-yard over the summer. Following the death of his father in 1924, finances got really tight, and Farnsworth quit college to work full time.

In the spring of 1926, nineteen-year-old Farnsworth found a temporary job with a visiting team of fundraising consultants who were helping to estab-lish the Community Chest in Salt Lake City. Farnsworth developed a rapport with the consultants, George Everson and Leslie Gorrell, and told them about his theory for an all-electrical television. Over time Everson and Gorrell came to be enthusiastic about Farnsworth's idea. The two decided to stake him with $6,000 (equivalent to over $62,000 in 2003) that Everson had earmarked for especially speculative investing in these "Roaring 20s."

Everson seems to have been the opposite of Abraham White, the sharp practitioner who promoted de Forest. Everson and Gorrell shared a fifty per-cent ownership of the partnership while Farnsworth kept half. With Everson giving him a shot at proving his dream, and $150 per month in salary, Farn-sworth married his sweetheart, Elma (known as Pem), and the two moved to Los Angeles, where Farnsworth would be close to the California Insti-tute of Technology, which was doing work in the technology that interested Farnsworth.

Farnsworth and Pem, who continued her mathematics studies to better serve as a laboratory assistant in the partnership, settled in Hollywood and began working. This was years before the advent of the prototypical "garage startup." With the team working with the curtains drawn and receiving pe-riodic after-hours visits from Everson dropping off crates of materials, and operating a generator in the garage that interrupted the neighbors' radio re-ception, the activities raised some suspicions. One summer day in 1926, amidst Prohibition, Farnsworth and Elma answered simultaneous rings at the front and rear doorbells. It was the police raiding the place looking for a still.[33]

Like many startups, the partnership quickly burned through its initial capital. The team moved to Everson's home town of San Francisco to search his network for additional capital. Then as now, these deals were often dis-cussed in fancy hotel dining rooms. Everson, aware that for all his genius, Farnsworth was still a nineteen-year-old farm boy with only a year of college under his belt, had to buy Farnsworth a suit and took him to breakfasts at the Fairmont Hotel to practice dining etiquette.[34] Soon they put together an im-pressive team of five investors led by W. H. Crocker, the son of the founder of Crocker Bank. Farnsworth estimated that he would need $25,000 to produce a recognizable, all-electrical television picture. The investors gave him that sum in exchange for 60 percent of the partnership.

In the fall of 1927, Farnsworth televised the first image, a black triangle. By the summer of 1928, he was ready to demonstrate this television to his backers by transmitting a part of a motion picture of the popular silent movie actress Mary Pickford combing her hair, presaging the market for films that television would create. The investors were impressed, but worried that it would take a "pile of money as tall as Telegraph Hill" to commercialize the device. Still, they carried on, and in March 1929 they incorporated as Television Laboratories, Inc., with half of the shares going to the trustees and half divided among the original partnership of Everson, Farnsworth, and Gorrell.[35] In August 1930, three-and-a-half years after it was filed, Farnsworth received a patent that broadly covered his system of television transmission and reception.

A major reason for the delay in receiving the patent stemmed from a company that did have a tall pile of money. RCA contested the Farnsworth patent application, claiming that their technology preceded Farnsworth's. It cost the new company $60,000 to fight the interference, but they won.

RCA had been following the patent submissions in television because one of its scientists, Vladimir Zworykin, had also been working on an all-electrical television system. At RCA, Zworykin, who had an excellent reputation for his prior work at Westinghouse, was researching the concept of all-electrical television similar to Farnsworth's. Farnsworth willingly accepted Zworykin's request to visit his San Francisco laboratory in order to prove his concept to the respected scientist, even though it entailed the risk of courting intense competition from RCA.

Farnsworth's contributions to television have largely been forgotten because of the efforts of RCA. Farnsworth was the first to demonstrate an all-electrical television system, but Zworykin and RCA were close behind with a somewhat different version. That Farnsworth's contribution has been largely forgotten is a result of the public relations efforts of David Sarnoff and RCA, who left few dollars unspent in associating the man and company with television in the minds of the public. That is not to say that Zworykin is undeserving of his reputation as the "Inventor of Television," but rather that Farnsworth is due far more attention than he has received. As historian Albert Abramson has pointed out, the current state of television owes more to Zworykin than to Farnsworth. Farnsworth's image dissector (the vacuum tube in the camera) had no storage cache, which "sowed the seeds of its own destruction," and Farnsworth's oscillite (picture tube) was not as good as Zworykin's kinescope. Neither Farnsworth's camera tube nor picture tube survived, whereas, Abramson writes, Zworykin's were clear forerunners of "modern camera and picture tube technology."[36]

There should be no denying Farnsworth's seminal role in the development of all-electrical television. RCA had to recognize the importance of Farnsworth's patents to television. For the first time in its history, RCA, that patent-pooler, had to look to somebody else's patents. In 1939, RCA acquired a nonexclusive license for Farnsworth's television transmitters and receivers and other technologies. In exchange, Farnsworth received similar license for similar technologies protected under RCA's patents.

Sidebar: Play It Again: History of Video Recorders

Until just recently, along Highway 101 in Redwood City, between San Francisco and Palo Alto, there were two large signs next to each other that were like extinguished beacons from two different consumer technologies. One sign marked the now empty headquarters of the failed Internet portal, Excite. The other, far larger sign, marked what had been the headquarters of a company called Ampex.

Ampex was founded in 1944 by an engineer named Alexander M. Poniatoff, who used his initials, with "ex" for excellence added at the end, to name the company. Four years after its founding, Ampex introduced the first American-made professional tape recorder. Singer and actor Bing Crosby, impressed with the prototype, ordered twenty of the machines when he realized that Ampex's audio-recording technology would allow him to prerecord radio shows.

As television began to take off, and national networks developed with affiliate broadcast stations sprouting across the country, Ampex turned its attention to developing technology for recording television. The still-small company was in competition with the mighty RCA to develop a new technology to record television. The technology then in use, the kinescope, was too costly for regular use. It seemed to Ampex and RCA that magnetic tape recording offered the most promising results. Working with a small team that included a young student named Ray Dolby, who would later go on to develop the eponymous noise reduction system, Ampex engineers beat RCA to the first practical video tape recorder (VTR).[37]

In April 1956, Ampex demonstrated its Mark IV VTR to a meeting of around two hundred CBS affiliates attending a broadcasting convention. The Mark IV recorded a speech given by a presenter and immediately played it back to the stunned audience. The company sold over one hundred machines, priced at $45,000 each (equivalent to over $300,000 in 2003), over the next four days, wildly exceeding their own market plan, which anticipated a market of only thirty machines, priced at $30,000, over three years.[38] At the time, Ampex, Hewlett Packard, and Varian Corporation ranked as the most significant companies in the young Silicon Valley.[39]

With the hefty price tag and with each machine larger than a deep freezer and side-by-side refrigerator, Ampex did not initially focus on the consumer market. Still, Ampex executives saw the distant potential for consumer markets. Ampex's president was quoted in the *Wall Street Journal* in 1956 as saying VTRs "might be mass-produced for home use by persons who want to see a program over and over again or want it recorded in their absence."[40] Two years later, a respected investment bank issued this amazingly prescient forecast: "It is impossible to estimate the potential market over the long run for video tape recording equipment. . . . [E]ventually small hand cameras using magnetic tape rather than film might be used by home and professional movie makers; video tape recorders may play these films back through conventional TV sets."[41]

For a while, Ampex managed to set the standard in VTR technology, accounting for three-fourths of all VTRs in use around the world in 1961.[42] Electronics companies such as Sony, Matsushita, and others in Japan, and Philips in Europe, began working with VTR technology, devising various improvements to reduce the size and price of their recorders. By that time, Japanese companies had become world leaders in solid state technology. Such circuitry would eliminate the need for vacuum tubes, which would reduce the size and cost of VTR machines while improving reliability. In 1961, anxious to get access to solid state technology, Ampex explored technology exchanges with Sony, which had its own experimental VTR program. However, the companies soon had a falling out. Three years later Ampex announced it had formed a joint venture to manufacture VTRs in Japan with another electronics company, Toshiba. By the middle of the 1960s, various Japanese competitors, along with Philips in Europe, were competing with Ampex for the video recording market.

By 1971 Sony had launched a cassette model (earlier recorders used unwieldy reel-to-reel tape) called the U-Matic, which used 3/4-inch tape. The product was still too expensive for most consumers, but it was used by schools and institutions and contained many of the design features that would soon be found in the popular Beta and VHS recorders.

E UNUM PLURIBUS?: HISTORY OF FILESHARING [43]

Before there was Napster, the popular music filesharing Web site, there were aliens—or there was the search for aliens. In 1998, a Berkeley computer science professor working with Berkeley's Space Sciences Lab devised a software program through which data from the world's largest single-dish radio telescope at Arecibo, Puerto Rico, could be parceled out in small (250 kb) chunks and processed by hundreds of thousands of idle PCs all over the world. Within two years, one of Berkeley's SETI projects, SETI@home, amassed two million volunteers who loaded screensavers onto their PCs that downloaded data from the telescope via the Internet, analyzed it, and reported back to a central server. The computers analyzed data for evidence of signals from potential alien civilizations, returning the results to a central clearinghouse. After its first fifteen months, SETI@home received the equivalent of 345,000 years' worth of computing time from its volunteers. The network of volunteers' computers was collectively the equivalent of a computer operating at approximately ten trillion calculations per second, about ten times faster than conventional supercomputers.

SETI@home used a distributed network, relying on computing capacity from its volunteers' unutilized PCs. Computing is said to be "distributed" when the programming and data that computers process are spread out over more than one computer, usually via a network. The computers can be of one type (for example, most SETI@home volunteers use PCs), but are more often a mix of desktop workstations, local area network servers, regional servers, Web servers, and other servers.

SETI@home and the famous filesharing service Napster both relied on distributed computers controlled by a central server. After downloading the Napster application, for example, a user could get access to music recorded in the MP3 format from other users who were online at the same time. Users searched for the name of an artist or a song title, received a list of available matches, and then downloaded the music directly from another user's hard drive. The files available depended on who was online at the time. Because the Napster server, like the SETI@home server, directed the activity, this model was sometimes called a "hybrid" peer-to-peer (P-to-P) model. A "pure" P-to-P model, by contrast, was one in which each party had the same capabilities and either party could initiate a communication session.

The phrase *peer-to-peer* refers to a set of technologies that enable the direct exchange of services or data between any groups of computers. Using P-to-P technology, some or all of the resources of any group of computers—such as processing cycles, cache storage, and disc storage for files—could be harnessed and directed.[44] P-to-P technology enables enterprises to take advantage of distributed computing resources—their own, or others'—by enabling a direct exchange of services between computers.

One advantage of P-to-P technology was illustrated by simulation batching, which showed how processing cycles could be shared. Workstations on a given network could access the computing resources of unutilized or lightly utilized machines. This allowed greater productivity, as teams that were in a work stage in which massive computing resources were needed could use the processing power from groups that were not using their machines so heavily at that moment. In this example, a data broker processed requests for computing resources by scanning its entire network for lightly used workstations. The broker sent batches of data to available machines for processing and received and assembled the processed data.[45] Corporate intranet users of P-to-P technology increased the utilization of their workstations, thus reducing the need to purchase more workstation or supercomputer processing power. Peer-to-peer computing could also be used to offload common server tasks such as file serving or virus protection to other peers on a network, allowing servers to focus on specific tasks such as handling business transactions.

Moreover, P-to-P technology had the potential to allow some network traffic to move from expensive corporate backbones to less expensive infrastructure such as switches, hubs, and routers. Other examples of immediate advantages to corporations using P-to-P technologies included filesharing and cycle sharing.

With P-to-P technologies, every computer could act as an "edge server" to those computers around it. Edge servers reduced the need to contact central servers and thus reduced traffic on expensive backbone lines by pushing data to servers located at the "edge of the Internet," closer to users. One advantage of P-to-P technology, advocated by Intel, was that it offered some of the advantages of edge servers. For example, when large files were downloaded across expensive pan-ocean backbones to distant locations, the systems registered the version in the satellite location and directed future exchanges of the file between satellite computers, thus eliminating the need to resend the large files over the costly backbone.

The concept and practice of P-to-P computing had been in existence for many years. For example, the Internet itself is essentially a pure P-to-P network. The Internet is a worldwide system of computer networks—a network of networks in which users at any one computer (or node) can, if they have permission, get information from any other computer.[46] The Internet was conceived by the Advanced Research Projects Agency (ARPA) of the U.S. government in 1969. The original aim was to create a network that would allow users of a research computer at one university to be able to communicate with research computers at other universities. An important feature of its design was its robustness; because messages could be routed or rerouted in more than one direction, the network could continue to function even if parts of it were destroyed.

The most widely used part of the Internet is the World Wide Web—all of the resources and users on the Internet that use the Hypertext Transfer Protocol (HTTP) devised by Tim Berners-Lee in the early nineties. Through the Web, users had easy access to millions of pages of information. Web usage greatly increased after 1993, when a program called Mosaic was released by the National Center for Supercomputing Applications (NCSA) at the University of Illinois in Urbana, Illinois. Mosaic was the first widely distributed graphical browser, or viewer, for the World Wide Web. Like the browsers that followed it, Mosaic was a client program that used HTTP to make requests of Web servers throughout the Internet on behalf of the browser user. Once Mosaic was available, the Web virtually exploded in numbers of users and content sites.

The explosion in popularity of the Web and concomitant increase in Web content created fertile markets for search engines and portals such as Yahoo!

and others that collected, sorted, and organized the fast-increasing content of the Web. These companies had few assets other than talented designers and engineers and increasingly powerful servers. The popular and financial successes of high-profile search engines and portals demonstrated the power of the client-server business model applied to the Internet.

CONCLUSION

As we have seen, innovation can come from anywhere. When most people, especially those close to Silicon Valley, think about the Innovation stage, they picture one or two smart and hardworking entrepreneurs working in a garage. After all, more than forty years before Bill Hewlett and Dave Packard founded HP in their garage, Marconi was busy in his parents' attic destroying the tyranny of distance. Innovation can come from a corporate hothouse too. Think of Edison and his teams of researchers striving to invent practical products and technologies. Innovation can also come from the individual talent who meets a supportive "angel" investor (think of Farnsworth) or a less scrupulous backer (like those encountered by de Forest).

While innovation can come from anywhere, there are certain common denominators to entering and transcending the next stage: Ascension. In the next chapter we look at the technologies we discussed that managed to survive the Innovation stage and see what it takes to enter and survive Ascension.

3 ASCENSION

IN JANUARY 1999, Northeastern University freshman Shawn Fanning wrote a P-to-P computer program that enabled him to trade MP3 files over the Internet with friends. Fanning called the program Napster, after a nickname earned him by his unruly hair, tamed with a buzz haircut. In the gold-rush atmosphere that existed as the NASDAQ was climbing to its peak, Shawn, and his uncle, John Fanning, quickly realized that the Napster program had far-reaching potential. The Fannings incorporated a company a few months later to distribute Napster, and began to inflict millions of tiny cuts on the (then) $14 billion recording industry.

Napster never really had a business model, that is to say a plan for making money. It also had the drawback of promoting copyright violations, which was the seed of its destruction (it was closed down by a judge). But what it had going for it was many, many people, at first mostly college and high school students but soon a wide variety of people, using the service to trade MP3 files over the Internet. It spread fast, like nothing ever before seen, and marked the Ascension of P-to-P technology and the Internet as a serious delivery channel of digitized content for consumers.

The way Napster was set up, the more people who gave the program access to their collections of digitized music, the more there was to share. At its peak, a mind-boggling amount of music was available from people around the world on Napster. It was a great example of a key element of the Ascension stage: network effects.

TUNING IN TO NETWORK EFFECTS

To transcend the Innovation stage, a particular technology must become more valuable as more people use it. A collection of benefits that accrue because of this is called network effects. Think of the fax machine. The first fax machine was not very useful. However, as more and more people purchased fax machines, fax users gained increased benefits from these devices because they could fax more and more people. This also happened with software. The network effects of the Microsoft Windows operating system became so compelling that Windows eventually ran over 90 percent of PCs around the world. Windows along with microprocessors from Intel became the so-called "Wintel" standard. A standard is a lot like a monopoly, except a standard is legal.

Another feature of network effects is that the benefits gained by users as more and more people adopt the technology or device can lead to so-called "lock-in," whereby the current technology becomes the standard and new and possibly even better technologies or devices are locked out of the market. This happens because many technologies become more useful as more people adopt them and because there is a cost to switching, whether from buying another device (why dump your eight-track tape player for a cassette player?) or, for more complicated devices, the time and sweat involved in learning how to operate something else.

Exclusivity is of course a nice thing to have at any stage. It is often present at the Innovation stage because almost by definition things at this stage are new. However, it can be short-lived. We saw in Chapter 2 how Marconi tried to use his company's brand and contracts to develop exclusivity where his technology did not provide it otherwise. Patents and copyrights can be very valuable because they reinforce legal exclusivity. That's why Microsoft and Intel made so much money from their "Wintel" standard.

This chapter shows how radio, recorded music, motion pictures, and television became big businesses, and how filesharing is poised to become one. Each had a different business model that supported its growth. The first big consumer application for filesharing was Napster, which like so many of its dotcom cousins did not make money. But Napster's undeniable success in attracting users did point to a yawning gap for downloaded music, a lacuna later filled by Apple's iTunes, and continues to point to a technology on the verge of Ascension through companies such as BitTorrent.

Radio, recorded music, movies, and television became big industries as each became popular and in turn became a more robust channel for delivery of content. As these industries grew, they came to encompass more types of content than each initially envisioned. For example, although radio started as a kind of audio telegram, it met its biggest success as a vehicle for attracting audiences by broadcasting recorded music (and delivering advertising to these audiences). Radio paid the recording industry for the use of this music and also served as a valuable promotional tool for the industry. The movie and television industries also became very symbiotic. And each benefited from a huge symbiosis with VCRs and DVD players, which created a demand for movies and TV shows on tape and DVD, generating new revenue.

MORE THAN WIRELESS TELEGRAPHY: RADIO BECOMES AN INDUSTRY

In the early years of the previous century, amateur radio enthusiasts, called "hams," tinkered with the technology. At that time, the military was the only large user of radio, and some hams, presaging their hacker great, great grandchildren, were accused of sending fake orders to admirals at sea.[1] In 1912 the government stepped in and mandated a licensing law to gain some control over the hams. Still, the nascent technology gained popularity, with radio clubs springing up in colleges and increasing numbers of home sets listening to the largely empty airwaves. The network effects of radio were beginning to spread.

A sure sign that radio had entered the Ascension stage was the battle involving commercial radio that took place in the early 1920s between amateur enthusiasts and "the interests," to use the phrase of the day, such as technology patent holders including RCA, Westinghouse, and AT&T. Consumer interest in radio technology had spread, and big companies were realizing the possibilities in building businesses around this interest. By the early 1920s, the amateur radio operators and broadcasters and the burgeoning commercial radio stations were increasingly bumping elbows in the ever more crowded airwaves. Also by this time, commercial radio had found its business model and was on its way to developing into a major medium of communication and entertainment.

It was a development that had long since caught the attention of American Marconi's chief inspector, David Sarnoff, a twenty-one-year-old Russian immigrant when Edwin H. Armstrong demonstrated his regenerative circuit to him on a cold January evening in 1914. Sarnoff was impressed as the two men sat huddled in a radio shack in New Jersey and pulled in signals from Ireland, Germany, San Francisco, and Hawaii. This and other developments in the technology convinced Sarnoff that radio had a future as a medium for commercial broadcast. In November 1916, Sarnoff wrote a memo to his boss at American Marconi. Sarnoff extrapolated from the ad hoc broadcasting efforts then under way with de Forest to form a business plan. Sarnoff began with the home market in mind. He wanted to make radio

> a "household utility" in the same sense as the piano or phonograph. The idea is to bring music into the house by wireless. . . .
>
> The receiver can be designed in the form of a simple "Radio Music Box" and arranged for several different wave lengths, which would be changeable with the throwing of a single switch or pressing of a single button.
>
> The "Radio Music Box" can be supplied with amplifying tunes and a loud-speaking telephone, all of which can be neatly mounted in one box. The box can be placed in the parlor or living room, the switch set accordingly and the transmitted music received. . . .
>
> The same principle can be extended to numerous other fields, as for example, receiving lectures at home which can be made perfectly audible; also events of national importance can be simultaneously announced and received. Baseball scores can be transmitted in the air. . . . This proposition would be especially interesting to farmers and others living in outlying districts removed from cities. By the purchase of a "Radio Music Box" they could enjoy concerts, lectures, music, recitals, etc., which may be going on in the nearest city within their radius.[2]

With World War I on the horizon, the commercialization of radio would be put on hold, much as happened with television in the early 1940s. Sarnoff bided his time.

When the United States entered World War I, the enthusiasts must have known that their hobby was about to change. Pranks to admirals would not be tolerated in wartime, and the same 1912 law that required broadcasters be licensed also allowed for the closure or seizure of civilian radio equipment "in time of war or public peril or disaster" at the discretion of the president. The day after the United States entered World War I, the hams were kicked off the air and had their equipment sealed. When the war ended, the amateurs returned. By this time the technology had grown on the back of developments fostered by the war. During the war, the U.S. government took over many of the critical patents for radio (and other technologies and services, such as telephone and the railroad and steel industries). The U.S. Navy, under the secretary of the navy, Josephus Daniel, and his assistant secretary, a young rising politician named Franklin Delano Roosevelt, assumed responsibility for the pool of radio patents under their stewardship.

Leading up to World War I, nationalist interest had directed the development of radio as a newly proven vital communication technology. At that time, British interests dominated commercial undersea telegraphy. Most undersea cable traffic traveled through Britain in one way or another, and British companies controlled the market for gutta-percha, the rubber insulation needed for undersea cables that was sourced from Malaysia. At the beginning of hostilities in 1914, Britain was able to cut German undersea cables, forcing that country to increase its reliance on the nascent wireless technologies. In fact, Armstrong earned his first royalties in 1914 from Telefunken, a German telecommunications company.

With the value and vulnerability of undersea cables in mind, there was much interest in Washington to control, or more closely monitor, the ownership of important wireless communications technologies. In 1919, this came to a head with General Electric's Alexanderson alternator, a vastly improved method for generating power for radios, and a technology that Marconi desperately wanted in order to improve its service. American Marconi's vice president Edward J. Nally was set to purchase $5 million worth of vital equipment from GE, primarily Alexanderson alternators and improved vacuum tubes, and wanted to negotiate a deal with GE to supply Marconi with exclusive rights to use the alternator. Owen D. Young, vice president of GE, conferred with Assistant Navy Secretary Roosevelt, who suggested that GE discuss the matter further with the Navy.

There was growing popular sentiment in the Congress for the nationalization of radio assets. This was a position also advocated by Navy Secretary Daniels. GE declined to sell the material to Marconi, citing U.S. government opposition to a deal that would send vital communications technologies to non-U.S. companies. Instead, GE, with the tacit approval of the U.S. government, offered to buy American Marconi's patents. The Marconi Company, facing the prospect of entering competition with GE and its superior technology, agreed to the sale. The patents of GE and American Marconi were combined into a single new company, the Radio Corporation of America. RCA, incorporated in October 1919, would be an American company, with

American management, American ownership (a maximum of 20 percent of its stock could be held by non-U.S. citizens), and a representative of the U.S. Navy invited to attend meetings of its board of directors. Most of the senior management of American Marconi assumed parallel positions in RCA: Owen Young became its chairman, Edward Nally became its president, and David Sarnoff, the technology manager who had earlier on recognized Armstrong's talent, became commercial manager.

The possibilities for radio occupied a much more prominent place in the minds of the RCA leadership. The company planned to build a state-of-the-art radio station in Rocky Point, Long Island. With Alexanderson alternators powering apparatuses featuring the best of the GE and Marconi patents, RCA was set to revolutionize radio communication. It was at this time that Sarnoff dusted off his prewar memo about the commercial possibilities of radio and presented a new version to Young, adding a particularly prescient forecast for Radio Music Box sales. At a price of $75 per set, Sarnoff predicted the following:

First Yr.	100,000 Radio Music Boxes	$ 7,500,000
2nd Yr.	300,000 Radio Music Boxes	22,500,000
3rd Yr.	600,000 Radio Music Boxes	45,000,000
Total		$75,000,000[3]

Sarnoff had been amazingly accurate. In its first year on the market, RCA sold $11,000,000 worth of sets. Its second-year results exactly matched Sarnoff's forecast. The third year of sales for radio sets exceeded Sarnoff's forecast by $5,000,000.

In 1920, RCA moved to further consolidate its position in the technology. AT&T, and its equipment subsidiary, Western Electric, controlled the rights to de Forest's audion. Wireless telegraphy, the primary business model for radio at that time, did not compete with AT&T's telephone business, but it was becoming easier to foresee conflicts between the two companies as radio evolved to transmitting voice. Antagonizing the holder of a central patent for radio technology could cause problems for RCA. To clear the way, Young gave AT&T about 10 percent of RCA's ownership in exchange for cross-licensing agreements concerning the patents on the vacuum tube that were held by AT&T. This brought together, within a single company, the Fleming tube and the de Forest audion, which had been built from that tube, as well as subsequent improvements to both technologies made by GE engineers, without fear of sticky litigation. As part of the agreement, signed in July 1920, and at the insistence of Sarnoff, AT&T granted RCA the right to establish and operate one-way wireless telephone transmitting stations. These would become radio broadcast stations.

Broadcast radio stations are precisely what Westinghouse, GE's and RCA's competitor, was already establishing. The company owned the Fessenden patents and had purchased Armstrong's patents on the regenerative circuit and superheterodyne, which had proven their usefulness in radio sets manufactured during the war when the patents had been taken over by the government. In 1920, Westinghouse began broadcasts from a station on the roof of its Pittsburgh factory. The company soon established broadcast stations on factory rooftops in Newark, New Jersey, and East Springfield, Massachusetts. The company aired music, news, prize fights, and even church services, all in a strategy to build demand for its radio sets.[4] Still, even though it had valuable patents and a nascent broadcasting operation, Westinghouse was not in a position to develop the technology, especially against the competition offered by RCA. Rather than slug it out, the two companies came to an agreement: in exchange for more than 20 percent of RCA's stock, Westinghouse transferred to RCA its transmitting patents and received from RCA use of its patents to manufacture equipment and sets for RCA. The deal made Westinghouse the largest corporate owner of RCA after GE.[5] RCA even bought out the radio interests of the United Fruit Company, which had been an early corporate adopter of the technology to communicate between its ships and plantations. The company sold its interest in a company that owned patents on radio antennas for a little over 4 percent of RCA stock.[6] RCA now had a clear field in which to develop the technology and business of radio.

A good sign that a technology is in the Ascension stage is that it attracts interest from companies in adjacent industries. We see this today with computer maker Apple's iTunes becoming a music, television, and movie distributor, and with cable companies offering phone service and phone companies offering video.

The network effects that marked the Ascension of radio (the "golden age of radio") were recognized by RCA and other companies by the 1920s. Broadcast radio networks were being developed. RCA was completing plans to launch its own radio network. The company believed that broadcasting content would help sell more sets. While General Electric and Westinghouse had been profiting under the arrangement in which they built radio sets for the burgeoning demand, and even the United Fruit Company had been content to watch its investment in RCA grow, AT&T felt it had been left out of the radio phenomenon. AT&T made radio transmission equipment, but few broadcast stations used AT&T's products, preferring to buy unlicensed equipment, much of which violated AT&T's patents.

Another reason was that AT&T realized early on the promise of so-called toll broadcasts, in which it could use its telephone call transmission assets and its business model as an entrée into broadcast radio. AT&T actually stalled customer requests for its Western Electric transmitters, telling buyers it would take many months or even years before their order could be filled, and instead offered to sell them time on the AT&T radio broadcast station WEAF.

At first, AT&T did not want to handle content. It preferred to handle radio in the same way it handled telephony, supplying the technology and letting customers supply the voices (content). But this proved unfeasible; with no content, you had no listeners, and therefore a station had little value. WEAF quickly developed content, at first largely composed of amateur musical performances by AT&T employees. On August 28, 1922, WEAF broadcast the first paid programming: a ten-minute presentation by the Queensboro Corporation to sell apartments in Jackson Heights, New York. It was said to be effective. Others, including department stores, followed.[7]

Radio was already big business. In 1922, Americans spent $60,000,000 (equivalent to over $660 million in 2003) on receiving sets. RCA made $11,000,000 selling GE and Westinghouse equipment. Broadcast radio was already RCA's biggest source of income, exceeding marine and transoceanic communications.[8] To get a piece of this Ascension action, the phone company went into the radio broadcasting business—with a vengeance.

AT&T sold its shares in RCA and set out to develop receiver technologies that would not infringe on RCA's patents. The move promised to set AT&T as a dangerous competitor to RCA. The competition was made more threatening by the important role that AT&T played in radio transmissions. Radio chain or network broadcasting relied on telephone lines for transmission of content. At that time, radio networks sent programming from one station to another over telephone lines.[9] As the battle heated up in 1921, more radio broadcasters were requesting telephone lines for the purpose of transmitting programming. Initially, AT&T discouraged its associated companies from connecting telephone lines with radio broadcasters. Soon it amended its decision to allow phone lines to noncommercial broadcasters. AT&T was about to embark on its own radio broadcast efforts. The company established WEAF in New York and WCAP in Washington, D.C. It seemed likely that AT&T could begin direct competition with RCA, using the phone company's equipment subsidiary, Western Electric, to manufacture receivers while AT&T built and operated broadcast stations. At this time, RCA began wiring its radio stations with telephone lines from Western Union and Postal Telegraph. The situation was not to the advantage of either AT&T, which wanted to continue its control of telephony in the United States and to whom radio broadcasting was becoming a large distraction, or to RCA, which wanted to establish itself as the prominent force in radio.

MAKING MONEY WITH RADIO

RCA and CBS each developed network structures that helped radio sustain itself through the Ascension stage. On November 15, 1926, RCA debuted its National Broadcasting Company (NBC) radio network. By January 1927, RCA had divided NBC into two networks: "NBC-Red" and "NBC-Blue." Already, sponsors paid for programs such as the "General Motors Family Hour," and advertisements were, for a time anyway, brief and dignified.[10] In 1926, RCA and AT&T came to a three-part agreement. RCA purchased AT&T's fledging network of radio stations, grouped under a company called Broadcasting Company of America. In effect, RCA paid one million dollars for the New York broadcast station WEAF, of which $800,000 was goodwill. RCA also agreed to use AT&T lines for broadcast transmission services (which had been denied them in 1921). And the companies agreed to cross-license their patents. This was a modification of the deal the companies had made in 1920. The result was that AT&T gave up its radio broadcast efforts and gained the telephone transmission business of RCA and its growing network of stations. In effect, each left the other to their respective territories. At this time, most radio stations were small and independent from either of the NBC networks or the new Columbia Broadcasting System (CBS), a fledgling radio network purchased in 1928 and developed by William S. Paley, initially as a vehicle for promoting the cigars manufactured by his family's company.

The business models used by NBC and its junior competitor CBS differed somewhat. NBC charged their affiliates for sustaining (that is, unsponsored) NBC-produced programming. The rate was $90 per hour of evening programming, later reduced to $50 per hour. NBC paid its affiliates to run sponsored network programs at a rate of $30 per evening hour, later increased to $50 per hour. The choice of whether to run the programming was left to the affiliates. Some affiliates found it more beneficial to run their own locally produced and sponsored programming than the network's fare.

CBS, under Paley, took a different approach. The network made all of its sustaining (unsponsored) programming available for free to its affiliates. The affiliate could use all, some, or none of the network's programming without charge. This was popular with cash-strapped affiliates facing the Depression of the 1930s. In exchange for this network largesse, CBS required an option on the affiliate's time for the network to run sponsored programming. Under this arrangement, CBS could sell time to sponsors without worrying about affiliates declining to run the sponsored show. In general, sponsors paid CBS at preestablished rates for each station that ran the sponsored programming. The revenue was often divided seventy-thirty between the network and the individual affiliate. The network incurred the production costs and transmission costs, including the AT&T line charges.[11] The Federal Communications Commission (FCC) would later force CBS to end its option arrangement with affiliates and force NBC to end its dual network structure.

JOCKEYING THE DISCS: RECORDS BECOME POPULAR

Well before there was the lovable spotted-eye dog shilling for Pets.com (remember that dotcom poster child?), there was "Nipper," the fox terrier with his head cocked listening to "his master's voice." Nipper was the symbol of the Victor Talking Machine Company. The company grew to become the leader in the record player industry. The trade name for its product, the "Victrola," came to signify any record player, whether made by Victor or one of its competitors. The company produced its own line of records (on the Red Seal label), operated its own orchestra, and signed exclusive recording contracts with the biggest names of the day, mostly opera stars, including Enrico Caruso. Victor had done very well for a while in the days before there was a radio in every home. In 1921, the company earned income of over $7 million from revenues of $47 million (equivalent to over $483 million in 2003). The next year its income dropped to $6.6 million, and in 1923 it earned only $1.2 million. The next year, Victor lost over $140,000. The tide had turned for the company, as phonograph sales plummeted in the face of popular broadcast radio and before the complement power of records and radio was fully exercised, powering both technologies out of the Ascension stage. In 1919 2.2 million phonographs were sold. In 1922, fewer than 600,000 were sold.[12]

Along with declining phonograph purchases, record sales plummeted. In 1925, Victor dropped the price of its $1.50 single-sided Red Seal records to 90 cents, and cut its $1.00 records to 65 cents. (We'll see this same action later with Universal Music Group cutting the prices of its CDs to $10 in 2003 in the face of a similar sales drop.) The price cuts did not work, and sales continued to fall.[13]

The industry despaired until technology offered a way out. In the mid-1920s, AT&T developed advanced technologies that dramatically improved the quality of recorded music, greatly reducing distortions that were common with the current recording technologies. Victor nearly arranged an exclusive license for the technology, but in the end, AT&T licensed it to almost every recording company in the country. Without exclusive access to this technology, Victor was forced to consider a merger or a joint venture. It chose the latter and joined with GE in offering combined phonographs and radio receivers. These featured the improved quality made possible by the AT&T technology. The machines went on sale in 1925. By 1926, Victor was back in the black, to the tune of reporting a $7.7 million profit for that year.[14]

With its improved performance came a run-up in Victor's share price, and with its newly valuable currency, the company looked to merge. By 1928, RCA, which had its own phonograph operation, and Victor began merger talks. When news of this leaked, Victor's shares rose from $50 to $145 and RCA's share from $85 to $380, buoyed by both bullish sentiments about the economies to be gained by joining such complements and, perhaps more important, the generally frothy atmosphere on Wall Street in late 1928.[15] By 1929 the deal was done, and RCA even purchased two large music publishers, going further upstream in the entertainment value chain.

Ten years later, CBS followed suit and purchased the Columbia Phonograph Company and Columbia Records in 1938. CBS would remain a distant second-place competitor to RCA until 1948, when CBS introduced the long-playing album, which recorded a little over twenty minutes of music per side. CBS even offered to license its LP technology to RCA, but the company declined because it had been sitting on its own improvement over the standard 78-rpm recordings, the 45-rpm record. Still, 45s were inferior to LPs (which turned at 33 rpm), and RCA had to submit to the LP technology.

Sidebar: Anatomy of a Record Label

Recording labels have had fundamentally the same value chain for much of the past one hundred years. Record companies, known as labels, manufacture and market CDs, tapes, digital downloads, and other mediums of music. Many record labels also make money by music publishing. Production, distribution, and publishing are often a part of the same corporate family. Labels seek out and sign musicians; record these artists (providing advice and guidance about both technical aspects and artistic content of the recordings); and publish, manufacture, package, and promote the resulting content, usually in the form of CDs but increasingly also in the form of newer consumption channels such as downloads and ringtones for mobile phones. In the first six months of 2005, digital music sales, including downloads, ringtones, and the like, accounted for 6 percent (or around $790 million) of overall sales for the industry.[16]

Perhaps the most important role played by the label is finding new talent to sign. This function can be considered a label's equivalent of research and development. Some have estimated that the industry spent around $2.5 billion on artist and repertoire (A&R) in 2004.[17] Record companies have extensive A&R departments, staffed with executives who search for new talent to sign. A&R representatives scout clubs and concerts, and listen to the tens of thousands of demo CDs sent to labels by hopeful musicians. A&R executives also oversee album and music video production, often in conjunction with independent producers, and create images for artists. Some music download sites, such as Beta Records and GarageBand, hope to attract A&R reps to the vast amount of reviewed music featured on those sites.

New artists signed by labels receive an up-front sum of cash, typically around $200,000 to $350,000, to cover recording costs of the first album, and another sum for video production. Some artists also can negotiate a separate deal for the publishing rights. Ninety percent of first albums fail to cover their costs. Because the odds are stacked against them, only a few artists get to record a second or third album for their labels. Even then, artists have to contribute some of the costs because the labels typically try to recoup some tour support and marketing costs against royalties.[18] Artists do not actually begin receiving royalties until record companies recoup their advances. Typical record contracts provide artists with a royalty of between 13 and 17 percent of sales revenue from their work.[19] Albums that sell 500,000 units are considered "gold" and sales of 1,000,000 units "platinum."

In addition to A&R people, record companies also keep on their payrolls successful producers who have extensive experience in producing albums. New artists' music is often quite "raw," and the work of high-quality producers can make or break an album. Producers might be either full-time employees of record companies or independent. Top-quality producers have high bargaining power with record companies and artists, and receive a cut of royalties going to artists. Interestingly, the advent of powerful but easy-to-use music software such as Apple's "GarageBand" application meant that very sophisticated-sounding music could be produced at home on personal computers without incurring the production costs just described.

Radio stations, which represent a good source of promotion for recording artists, add only three or four songs to their playlists in any given week. Thus record labels spend considerable sums for promotion. For a standard release, typical marketing expenses run to $100,000 per album and can exceed $500,000 for a major artist release. In addition, music videos are typically produced at an additional cost, ranging from $70,000 to $100,000 for new and midlevel artists: all for the extremely unlikely chance of creating a hit record.

The largest record labels are also music publishers. Unlike record labels, which essentially earn revenues only from the sale of CDs (or other media), the typical music publishing company has a more diversified revenue stream. These revenue sources include performance income, earned when its songs are played on the radio, on television, in concert, in nightclubs, and so on, and synchronization or transcription fees, earned from the use of music in films, television shows, commercials, and so on. Typical television licenses can earn between $1,000 and $3,000 for the use of a song in a television program, while typical film fees range from $15,000 to $75,000 and higher and typical television commercial fees go from $25,000 to $500,000 and higher. However, these fees can vary widely depending on the popularity and current market value of a song. In addition, publishers earn fees from the sale of sheet music and songbooks.

YOUR BEST ENTERTAINMENT: MOVIES BECOME BIG BUSINESS

Nickelodeons were nice, but movies really became a big business when more than one paying customer could watch the film at the same time, and generated the kind of growth that marks Ascension. The transition to exhibiting movies on a screen was eased by the ready availability of vaudeville theaters, many of which became movie houses.

New industries tend to develop as vertical industries out of necessity. Think of the PC industry. When it was new, PC makers had to supply all of the elements of the PC themselves because horizontal industries providing elements such as software and microprocessors for the PC had not yet developed.

Movies developed a little differently. The motion picture industry entered the Ascension stage as a horizontal industry. That is to say that the same companies did not own production, distribution, or exhibition. This changed.

In the early days of the industry, filmmakers sold their motion pictures outright to exhibitors. Prices ranged from $10 to $25 per hundred-foot film. This arrangement proved wasteful for exhibitors, who saw demand by a given theater's local audience for a given motion picture decline well before the print wore out. Exhibitors began to exchange films among themselves, and by 1903 third-party film exchanges had appeared. Distributors rented films to exhibitors, usually charging 25 percent of the film's purchase price. A key element of success for nickelodeons was audience turnover. Exhibitors preferred short films and changed them frequently. Film distributors suffered from many illegal tactics practiced by exhibitors, including duplication of the film print and "bicycling," a practice in which one exhibitor rented a film and in concert with other neighboring exhibitors staggered showings so the print could be bicycled to the other theaters.

In 1909, the MPPC began to use its monopoly power to bring order to the industry. During the time that the motion picture industry was dominated by the MPPC, movie releases were generally handled in one of two ways: either by states' rights or by road show. Under the states' rights method, motion picture makers sold their films by territory to an individual exhibitor. Because films were sold according to their length to make as much money as possible, exhibitors would show the motion picture until the print wore out from use. Under the states' rights distribution method, the producer made money on the initial sale of the film print, but the exhibitor made more money, charging viewers a nickel a showing for as long as the print was usable.[20]

An alternative distribution model was known as road show distribution. Under this method, motion picture producers retained their films and contracted directly with theater owners for exhibition. These showings were billed as special theatrical engagements, and audiences were usually charged more than five cents for admission. The revenue generated by road show exhibitions was retained by the motion picture maker. Some films utilized both methods of distribution, first using road show exhibitions for profitable urban markets (the so-called A theaters) and then selling prints under states' rights into secondary markets (the so-called B theaters).

A number of independent film producers competed with the MPPC. These independent filmmakers often produced movies that were considered better than the standardized fare issued by the MPPC. For example, independents initiated the "star system," in which favorite actors were publicized to increase demand for their films. The MPPC preferred to keep their players more anonymous to better interchange them in movies. Independents also led the way toward longer feature films that brought in wider audiences than the short films playing in nickelodeons. By the time the MPPC was dissolved, several independents had established themselves as forces in the industry.

An alternative system of motion picture distribution was pioneered by W. W. Hodkinson, a one-time employee of the General Film Company, the distribution arm of the MPPC. Under Hodkinson's system, a film distributor would buy exclusive rights to a film and return 65 percent of the box office revenue to the filmmaker. The distributor kept 35 percent of the receipts and handled film distribution and marketing. Hodkinson even envisioned the distributor advancing financing to producers. Such a system could appeal to cash-strapped independent motion picture producers (those not associated with the MPPC). Although Hodkinson's system met with success when tested in San Francisco in 1911, the MPPC did not support the distribution method. Hodkinson was dismissed from his job with General Film.

Undeterred, Hodkinson formed the Progressive Company in California to contract with and distribute the films of independent filmmakers. These included such future standouts as the Famous Players Company, founded by Adolph Zukor, and the Jesse L. Lasky Feature Play Company, cofounded by Lasky, his brother-in-law Samuel Goldfish (later changed to Goldwyn), and film director Cecil B. DeMille. In 1914, Hodkinson expanded his company to the East Coast and changed the name to Paramount Pictures Corporation. Under the Paramount organization, the distributor enjoyed more power than filmmakers. Disagreements developed between Zukor and Hodkinson. As early as 1915, Zukor realized the value of tight integration of motion picture production and distribution and exhibition. Zukor grew to resent the imbalance of power, and he tried to extricate himself from his contract with Paramount. Hodkinson refused. In what amounted to a hostile takeover, Zukor and Lasky gained control over a majority of Paramount stock and ousted Hodkinson. On July 19, 1916, Zukor and Lasky merged their companies with Paramount, creating the Famous Players-Lasky Corporation, a motion picture production and distribution company valued at $12.5 million.

Famous Players-Lasky and Paramount, under their new direction, were able to exercise considerable power in the United States motion picture industry. The companies' market power allowed them to engage in several practices that were profitable but ultimately deemed to be illegally anticompetitive. The most infamous of these were block booking and blind booking. Block booking involved licensing one feature or group of features on the condition that the exhibitor will also license other features released by the distributor during a given period. Under block booking, exhibitors had to accept films in blocks, often getting one likely hit along with several less attractive features. Block booking ensured that motion picture producers sold their entire inventory. Along with block booking, motion picture producers often forced exhibitors to accept blind booking, whereby exhibitors had no information or only scant information about the films they were accepting for exhibition.

The events described next show how regulatory forces can have an impact on entertainment industries. Because Hollywood felt the sharp end of government regulation in the 1920s through the late 1940s, it has been active in expressing its views in Washington (read lobbying) compared with the technology industry, which until recently disdained lobbying and therefore has had to play catch up as its regulatory interests, particularly regarding copyright protections, diverged from those of Hollywood.

In 1921, the United States Federal Trade Commission filed a complaint charging Famous Players-Lasky with restraint of trade by forcing exhibitors to buy unwanted films through the practice of block booking. Although the case focused on block booking, the investigation also brought studio ownership of theaters under scrutiny. The FTC accused Famous Players-Lasky of using theater acquisition—and the threat of theater acquisition—to intimidate exhibitors into block-booking arrangements for Paramount-distributed motion pictures.

In 1927 the FTC concluded that block booking was indeed an unfair trade practice and issued a cease and desist order for block booking on July 9, 1927. The three respondents—Famous Players-Lasky Corporation, Adolph Zukor, and Jesse L. Lasky—were given sixty days to comply with the findings or to provide the FTC with written explanations. After two extensions, Famous Players-Lasky issued a report in which they disputed the FTC findings. The FTC rejected Famous Players-Lasky's compliance report in April 1928 and resolved to go after the larger industry.

On April 27, 1928, the Department of Justice filed two antitrust cases, later combined into one suit in 1930. The government accused ten motion picture companies, including Paramount and Famous Players-Lasky Corporation, of monopolizing 98 percent of domestic distribution. In October 1929, the Federal District Court in New York City issued a judgment that satisfied neither the government nor the defendants, and both sides appealed to the Supreme Court (a situation that would repeat seventeen years later in the Paramount case). In the Supreme Court decision delivered on November 25, 1930, the ten Hollywood distributors were found guilty of violating antitrust law, and block booking was identified as the fundamental problem.

The reforms mandated by the Supreme Court were not enforced due to the turmoil the industry suffered in the economic depression of the 1930s. Instead the motion picture producers reached an agreement with the Roosevelt administration that would allow the industry to continue its practices, including block booking, until its financial situation improved. This would continue until the industry was again sued by the United States government.

In 1938, the United States government again filed suit against the major movie studios. However, in 1940 both sides reached a consent decree in which the studios agreed to limit block booking to no more than five films per block and to completely eliminate blind booking in favor of trade showings, in which films were shown to prospective buyers in advance of orders. The studios were allowed to retain their theaters in exchange for a commitment not to expand theater holdings without federal approval.

When the consent decree expired in 1943, the government refused to extend the decree under the previous terms. Instead, it sought to divorce the exhibition of films from distribution within three years. The government also sought to prohibit film distributors from acquiring any theater interests and required divestiture of theaters as might be necessary to restore competition in communities where exhibitors had theater-operating monopolies. The issue was argued before the Supreme Court in February 1948, and in three months the court handed down its ruling. A majority of justices sided with the government, calling some of the studios' practices "bald efforts to substitute monopoly for competition." The Supreme Court again found block booking illegal but remanded to a lower court other issues, including studio ownership of theaters—the hallmark of studio vertical integration and the crux of the government's complaint.[21]

Some studios vowed to continue to fight the issue. However, one major studio named in earlier cases, but not the most recent Supreme Court case, Howard Hughes's RKO, announced it would spin off its theater chain from its studio operations. Paramount, wishing to end the costly and distracting legal battle, followed suit, entering into an agreement with the Justice Department to divest its theater operations in February 1949.

By the time the Paramount case was settled, the U.S. film industry had entered a prolonged downturn. During this period, movie attendance dropped by half, four thousand theaters closed, and studio profits fell dramatically.[22] Studios also had to contend with what they perceived as a major technological challenge in the form of television.

THEN THERE WERE THREE: THE TELEVISION INDUSTRY

The development of television was stalled during World War II, and regular commercial broadcasts had to wait until after the war. When the development of television networks picked up again, the movie studios saw only a new competitor. In 1939 there were approximately only two hundred television sets in the United States (mostly located in New York City, where the only broadcast took place). However, by 1947, as technical standards for television were decided, the number of sets in the United States had risen to 14,000, and it reached 172,000 in 1948. The following year, there were one million sets in the country, and that figure quadrupled by 1954.[23]

In a time before Bruce Springsteen could record a song called "57 Channels (and Nothin' On)," there was room for only three television networks in the United States—but four network broadcasters vying for survival through the Ascension stage. The first two television broadcasters on the air were National Broadcasting Company (NBC), a radio network owned by RCA, and the Columbia Broadcasting System (CBS), a competing radio network, both of which had begun occasional television broadcasts by 1939. The third entrant was the DuMont network, owned by Allen B. DuMont Laboratories, a small maker of cathode ray oscilloscopes and television sets. In 1938 DuMont sought to vertically integrate along the television value chain, like its larger competitor RCA—to manufacture television sets, to eventually broadcast content, and to own stations. NBC and CBS, ahead of the much smaller DuMont, initiated regular television broadcast services in July 1941, but, as noted earlier, most television broadcasting and development was halted during World War II.

After the war, both NBC and CBS were able to use their skills in programming, sales, and marketing in radio to gain an early lead in the nascent television market. Some observers believe that the FCC, in an effort to bring television to the broadest possible audience in the country, at the expense of a truly competitive marketplace, favored the big two broadcasters. Technical decisions about allocating the superior VHF and the then experimental UHF broadcast spectrums (NBC and CBS possessed a larger number of stations operating in the VHF frequency while television sets at the time could not even receive UHF signals without an additional receiver) seemed to limit the marketplace to two dominant networks with room for one weaker network.

By the end of World War II, American Broadcasting Company (ABC), a radio network formed in 1943 with radio stations gained through the FCC-imposed divestment of one of RCA's two radio networks, entered the television broadcasting market. ABC soon merged with United Paramount Theaters (UPT), a chain of movie theaters divested from Paramount as a result of earlier consent decrees. The merger gave ABC increased financial muscle compared with the DuMont network. Coincidentally, Paramount was a minority investor in DuMont, a fact that presented the erstwhile network with little financial help and much negative regulatory baggage. The television market in the United States at that time could not sustain four national broadcast networks. The DuMont network closed in 1955. Under the status quo that resulted, with ABC eventually gaining a status commensurate with CBS and NBC, the "big three" networks grew to be very powerful. At the height of their power in the 1960s, these three networks accounted for 90 percent of all television viewing in the country.

IT'S GOOD TO SHARE?
THE EMERGENCE OF PEER-TO-PEER SERVICES

Napster proved the viability of a consumer peer-to-peer channel delivered via the Internet. Napster grew so fast that it was nearly born into the Ascension stage. While it did not survive the Innovation stage, it did pave the way for P-to-P technology itself to enter Ascension.

Napster was a computer program that enabled users to search for file titles (for example, song titles) on the computers of other users who had the same Napster program on their computers and were logged on to Napster.com at the same time. The Napster software displayed information about the files available for copying, such as the connection speed of the fellow user and bit rates at which MP3 files were encoded (a proxy for sound quality), and allowed users to search other logged-on users' computers for MP3 files by file name and artist name. Once a user identified a desired song, he or she could download it from the other user's PC with relative ease. Songs could be downloaded in a matter of minutes. Once downloaded, a song could be played on a user's PC on demand, or, with the right hardware, transferred to a CD (a process called "burning") and then played on any traditional CD player. Software programs to play MP3 files on a PC were freely available over the Internet and were distributed by software vendors Microsoft, MusicMatch, Nullsoft-Winamp (an AOL-Time Warner company), and RealNetworks, who together had distributed hundreds of millions of copies. Napster was a classic Internet-age "infomediary"; while it did not own MP3 files, the software to play them, or even the MP3 format, it afforded individuals around the world the ability to connect their music with each other.[24]

In November 1999, two weeks before Napster had even officially launched as a company, the battle lines had been drawn. The 2.0 beta version of its software had already been distributed among online music aficionados. "I love it," wrote Marc Geiger of ArtistDirect, a competitor digital music site, "it's totally community oriented and a pass-the-music play. It argues totally for the subscription model we have been yapping about." A *Wired* magazine article reported that "fans like Napster because it combines existing elements of the online music experience into a single application that allows people to talk about what music they like and trade files."[25] When Napster finally launched, the music industry was ready. The Recording Industry Association of America (RIAA), an industry group representing the major record companies, fired the first shot. The RIAA sued Napster for promoting music piracy just two days after the Website launched. Napster's official response to the suit announcement was instructive, capturing the company's vision in a nutshell. "We are about new artists, unknown music . . . about community and sharing," said then-Napster CEO Eileen Richardson.[26] By December 1999, less than a year after the program had been written, a group of eighteen irate record companies filed suit to close down the company.

From the recording industry's perspective, Napster was about the piracy of copyrighted material—recorded songs—and industry members set about suing the company out of existence. Whatever it was about, Napster still did not have a business model. As the dotcom boom finally started to turn to bust in March 2000, Napster, attracting millions of users, also attracted millions of dollars from venture capitalists; $15 million from the venture capital firm of Hummer Winblad Venture Partners, to be specific. As part of the deal, Hummer Winblad partners Hank Barry, an attorney who had headed the technology practice of the Palo Alto, California, law firm of Cooley, Godward and prior to that worked in the entertainment practice of the white shoe law firm of Paul, Weiss, Rifkind, Wharton & Garrison in New York, and John Hummer joined the board of directors, with Barry assuming the role of Napster's interim CEO. While Napster's valuation details were not made public, industry observers speculated that it was substantial, approaching at least several tens of millions of dollars. Barry soon set out championing Napster's legal defense in the courts as well as in the court of public opinion. In a speech at Stanford's Graduate School of Business in late 2000 he underlined that Napster's original vision had still not changed: "We are a membership and community service for sharing music, not a music subscription service," he pointed out, making a virtue of the company's inability to develop a paying business. Barry also implied that what Napster was doing was legal and fell under the "fair use" doctrine of copyright law. He also sought to portray Napster as under attack primarily because it threatened the record companies' stranglehold on distribution.[27]

Through March 2001, when Judge Marilyn Hall Patel effectively ordered it to shut down, Napster continued to receive significant press coverage and popularity even though it had still to make any money. With no advertising or marketing, Napster's user base had grown from a few thousand to tens of millions. The number of files available through its service had grown from tens of thousands to hundreds of millions.

The record industry was successful in decapitating Napster, but like the hydra from mythology, several more filesharing services sprang up in its place, each more difficult to stop than Napster had been. In fact, the record companies took to suing fileswappers (see further on) in a move that was sure to earn them enmity from their customers for years to come.

In addition to Napster, a popular application called Gnutella offered an example of a pure P-to-P model. Gnutella was a real-time search-and-file-share Internet application that enabled users running Gnutella software to search for and download files from other Gnutella users.

Gnutella was developed by Justin Frankel and his colleagues at Nullsoft, an AOL subsidiary. Earlier, Nullsoft had developed the popular Winamp, the leading branded MP3 player for Windows, and SHOUTcast, an MP3 streaming audio system. When AOL announced its $86 million acquisition of Nullsoft, founder and president Frankel said, "Working with America Online will let us globally extend the use of our technologies through its Internet brands. In addition, having access to America Online's tremendous resources and infrastructure will let us focus our efforts on what's really important: making cool software."[28] He was right. Soon after Gnutella was posted on the AOL/Nullsoft Web site, the program was pulled following complaints by Time Warner's Gerald Levin. Still, the program proliferated and became freely available from various sources on the Web. Unlike hybrid P-to-P programs, Gnutella and other pure P-to-P programs do not use a central server.

This is also true of the RIAA's more recent bête noire, KaZaa. This pure P-to-P service was organized in the Netherlands, and the servers it uses are located outside of the United States.

A newer company on the P-to-P scene is BitTorrent, the brainchild of a young programmer named Bram Cohen. The company is giving some movie studios headaches because the technology can be used to quickly share large files—such as movies—over the Internet. BitTorrent software breaks large files into smaller pieces. BitTorrent users (peers) download the pieces from each other and upload those that they already have to peers that request them. BitTorrent software directs peers to others with the best network connections for their requested pieces of a given file. However, this does not occur without users leaving digital fingerprints, which could make them subject to litigation if they trafficked in copyrighted materials.

Sidebar: Dead Ends

Some compelling technologies do not make it past the Innovation stage. For example, Philo Farnsworth, despite his genius and his patient and even helpful backers, was not able to overcome RCA with its deep pockets and its superior technology.

But superior technology is not enough to guarantee success, either. Video aficionados enjoy arguing about whether VHS or Beta was actually the superior standard. What is clear is that Sony's Betamax standard lost against Matsushita's VHS. Sony had early if incomplete success in video recording technology with its U-Matic video tape recorder (VTR). Most VTR research in Japan coalesced around the Sony and its technology standard. Japanese video recording technology leaders Sony, Matsushita, and JVC signed a cross-licensing agreement to share VTR patents in 1970. European leader Philips did not join.

The Sony-Matsushita-JVC deal proved unworkable for the participants. In particular Sony, which was farther along in developing a marketable product than Matsushita, felt that its partner had slowed its market entry. For its part, Matsushita felt that Sony enjoyed unfair advantage in their agreement. When Sony introduced a new home VTR, now called a videocassette recorder (VCR), with a 1/2-inch tape, and invited Matsushita to join it in propagating a new standard, Matsushita dragged its feet and eventually declined. In 1975 Sony went ahead and launched its Beta-standard VCR. The next year, Matsushita launched its own VCR with the VHS standard.

Both Beta and VHS were based on the earlier U-Matic technology, and neither was clearly technologically superior to the other. However, each was incompatible with the other, meaning if you had a Beta tape, you could not play it in a VHS VCR, and vice versa. Different observers have various opinions about the relative merit of the technical specifications for Beta and VHS. However, what is certain is that, initially, VHS tapes offered longer recording times and VHS VCRs were a little cheaper. These turned out to be powerful advantages. First mover Sony's Beta format enjoyed production and market share leads from 1975 through 1977, but by the next year, VHS had outstripped Beta in production and market share. In 1981, 6,478,000 VHS-format VCR units were produced compared with 3,020,000 Betamax units.[29] VHS-standard VCR sales continued to outpace Beta sales until the standard finally withered.[30]

Another would-be format that did not get far was the videodisc. Several different videodisc technologies were developed separately by MCA, in partnership with Philips, Pioneer, and RCA, among others. By this time, RCA was a shadow of the company that had loomed so prominently in the story of radio told earlier. MCA, however, was much more powerful in entertainment in the second half of the 1970s, when its videodisc technology was introduced to consumers. MCA owned Universal Studios, which it acquired in 1962. As we will see, this is the studio that, along with Disney, tried to sue the VCR out of existence. In the late 1970s, an MCA-backed technology would be a force to be reckoned with.[31]

The two videodisc systems used different technologies to read an image from a plastic disc. The RCA system worked much like a record player, with its discs being read by a needle in the groove. The MCA system, developed in partnership with Philips, was more sophisticated, using a laser to read a disc, much like a CD. The MCA-Philips videodisc players were more expensive, costing about 1.5 times the price of the RCA "selectavision" system. Neither system could record; they could play only what was prerecorded on the discs. While this was an obvious drawback to the videodisc systems compared with VCRs, which could record, RCA and MCA hoped that three things would enable the systems to be competitive against the nascent VCR competitors. One was the lower price of their prerecorded discs, about $25, which was less than the price of a blank VCR tape at the time. Second was the ease of use of the videodisc systems compared with complex VCRs. Third were the superior features of the MCA-Philips device, unfortunately named

"DiscoVision," which allowed users to scan and freeze-frame movies and offered a better quality picture.

Since you probably never had a videodisc player in your living room (condolences if you did), you can guess the outcome. Videodisc technology suffered from two drawbacks: they could not record, and they were mired in the "start-up" or "chicken-and-the-egg" problem. Since videodiscs could not record, they could not be used for the first popular function of the VCR—time-shifting. Recording television broadcasts such as favorite shows or games that otherwise would have been missed was the "killer application" or popular use that drove sales of VCRs. If the videodisc had been introduced before the VCR, it might have found a market for a while, because some movie titles were slowly becoming available on disc. However, with VCRs and their recording functionality already on the market, it was very difficult for videodiscs to compete. As difficult as it was to overcome in 1977 when MCA launched its system, it was nearly impossible to overcome when RCA finally launched its videodisc system in 1981. Philips may have learned its lesson when it managed to avoid the start-up problem for its music CD technology a few years later. Partially through the power of vertical integration (it owned 50 percent of the Polygram record label), Philips was able to coordinate the launch of CD players with the release of music on CDs by its and other's labels.[32]

Then there is the problem that comes from doing well enough. Marconi's network of base stations performed well enough and its coherer worked well enough that it did not see the need to stay on top of the cutting edge of radio technology. Perhaps because they were rather financially conservative and valued steady predictable cash flow above innovation, Marconi's management, from both its U.K.-based parent and American Marconi, were slow to take advantage of the significant improvements in radio technology that were being made by other inventors and seemed content (until it was too late) to stick with using radio for telegraphic communications.[33] In doing so, they missed a great opportunity to think differently about their technology and create a whole new industry. Instead, Marconi left commercial radio to RCA.

CONCLUSION

Compliments are nice, but in technology complements are better. The technologies we have looked at in this chapter benefited from the power of complements to propel them into and through the Ascension stage. (The jury is still out as to whether P-to-P will make it to Prosperity, but it looks very promising.)

The success that goes with Ascension often provokes fear in those who at first glance seem to have the most to lose from the Ascending technology. Ironically, it is often those would-be complements that have a lot to gain from the Ascending technologies. But as we will see, in the past these complements had to be led to water more than once before they finally drank. Complements were reluctant to embrace the ascending technologies because they were fearful of the impact on themselves and their established ways of doing business.

4 FEAR

BEGINNING IN 1976 movie studios tried their hardest to kill the videocassette recorder (VCR). A group of studios led by Universal set their sights on Sony, which had been the first to market with its ill-fated Betamax video recorder. The studios tried to sue Sony, claiming that the device encouraged copyright infringement, and sought to have VCRs hobbled by blocking their recording functions, a move that certainly would have made the devices far less popular with consumers. In what would have been a tragedy for the studios, they came within a single vote of winning their case before the United States Supreme Court and making the VCR and its successor the DVD player illegal. When you consider that movie sales and rentals for home use became significant moneymakers for studios as soon as VCRs became ubiquitous and that by 1998 video sales and rentals had accounted for half of the studios' annual revenues, you can see how foolhardy the studios had been in opposing VCRs.

The movie studios feared and tried to destroy the nascent VCR technology because they were shortsighted. This is a classic response for companies or indeed industries in the Fear state: they fail to recognize complements and instead think only about killing what they perceive as a threat.

In this chapter, we look at how our industries stumbled through the Fear stage, time and again shooting themselves in the foot by seeing new complements only as competitors and failing to exploit opportunities that sometimes should have been obvious.

As mentioned in earlier chapters, these technologies at least had the opportunity to go through the first two stages of the road to Prosperity (Innovation and Ascension) without bumping into each other and thus were able to get a foothold. Today, in our increasingly converged world, many innovative technologies do not have that luxury. Instead, they bump up against more established technologies and industries that seek to inhibit or destroy the nascent technologies. Lately, the weapon of choice has been patents or copyrights.

Right now, there is a lot of shouting over the terms of protection, for copyrights in particular. If you just read the headlines, this may seem like an arcane concern. But it isn't. It directly affects consumers, because if the balance between property owners (copyright holders) and property users (consumers or even other companies) tips too far to one side, consumers pay too much and innovation gets stifled; if it tips too far to the other side, investors are not sufficiently rewarded and innovation again gets stifled. That is why it is important to have at least a passing familiarity with the main tools of intellectual property protection. See Appendix B for a discussion of copyrights and patents.

THE SONNY BONO LAW:
I GOT YOU BABE FOR ANOTHER TWENTY YEARS

In 1976, Congress extended the term of copyright protection from twenty-eight years, renewable once, to the life of the author plus fifty years. In the late 1990s severe copyright laws that favored the property rights interests of content owners started coming out of Congress. In 1998, entertainment companies vigorously lobbied Congress for two pieces of legislation that affected their IP property rights. One extended the length of American copyrights, enacted under the Sonny Bono Copyright Term Extension Act (CTEA), introduced by Senator Orrin Hatch (R-Utah) and named for the late Congressman Sonny Bono (R-Calif.), a former hit songwriter and performer who gained fame in the late 1960s with his former wife, Cher.

Under the Sonny Bono CTEA, Congress extended the term of copyright to life of the author plus 70 years and with respect to "works made for hire" 95 years after publication or 120 years after creation, whichever expires first. Opponents sued the government, claiming that the extension was a violation of the First Amendment of the Constitution, which protects free speech.[1] The challenge was heard by the Supreme Court, which in January 2003 found that the Congress had the authority to set the terms for copyright protection, and the Supreme Court would defer to the Congress's determinations on copyright terms. The Court found that the First Amendment does not limit the Congress's power to extend copyright terms.

Digital Millennium Copyright Act

The second, and far more controversial piece of legislation, the Digital Millennium Copyright Act (DMCA), was also enacted in 1998. This law declared that "no person shall circumvent a technological measure that effectively controls access to a work protected" by copyright. The DMCA made it a crime not only to copy a protected work, but to de-encrypt an encrypted work without authorization. The law also contained stipulations that made it illegal to manufacture, release, or sell any tools, hardware, or software designed to circumvent encryption of a copyrighted work. This is known as the "anti-circumvention" provision of the law. The DMCA contained provisions that gave ISPs and Web hosts "safe harbor" from copyright infringement claims if they implemented notices and removal procedures to eliminate infringing content. (Indeed, YouTube and other video posting sites claim protection under this safe harbor provision and do remove copyrighted content when required.) However, the law had the potential to make it illegal to manufacture and sell much of the software and hardware that technology companies hoped would make media over the Internet a common application and at the same time help pull them out of recession. In January 2003, under the DMCA, a federal judge ordered Verizon Communications (a Regional Bell Operating Company formed from the mergers of Bell Atlantic, Nynex, and GTE) to reveal to a record industry trade group the identity of an Internet subscriber suspected of making available unauthorized copies of several hundred songs. This marked a departure for recording companies that in the past had focused their legal efforts against online filesharing services such as Napster and others. Verizon appealed the decision and won the appeal, and in October 2004 the U.S. Supreme Court declined to hear the case. This victory for Verizon offered only a very thin reed to its customers with privacy concerns.

Consumer Broadband and Digital Television Promotion Act

In March 2002, United States Senator Ernest F. Hollings (D-S.C.), chairman of the Senate Commerce Committee, and five cosponsors, introduced legislation called the Consumer Broadband and Digital Television Promotion Act.

The bill required that new hardware and software, from CD players to television sets to computers, block unauthorized copying of copyrighted works. It would have movie studios, record labels, and others attach digital tags to a movie, song, or album that would encode rules about how it could be played, viewed, or copied on devices such as computers or digital TVs. Manufacturers and content owners would have a year to agree on technology to enforce these rules; after that, the Federal Communications Commission could impose a standard. It would then be illegal to manufacture devices that did not implement that standard. Hollings said, "I believe the private sector is capable, through marketplace negotiations, of adopting standards that will ensure the secure transmission of copyrighted content on the Internet and over the airwaves. . . . But given the pace of private talks so far, the private sector needs a nudge."[2] The bill's supporters said the legislation was designed to stimulate the growth of high-speed Internet access and digital television.

Supporters argued that consumers have been slow to adopt services such as broadband Internet access because there was not enough programming and content, and copyright owners will not provide that content online until they are sure people cannot make and distribute unauthorized copies. But opponents of the bill feared it would grant copyright owners too much control over how consumers use technology. Another concern for some critics was that the provisions of the Act would have imposed rules on computer design that could seriously impair the PC industry by prohibiting it from incorporating technologies that consumers would want to enable them to consume media such as CDs and DVDs on PCs.

These laws are meant to protect the legitimate interests of content owners in an age when their property is at increasing risk of theft from technologies borne of the forces discussed in this book. However, the laws are sweeping in their powers and can have seriously damaging consequences (intended and unintended) on other industries, such as PC makers, and on American society as a whole. The DMCA, and in particular its anticircumvention provisions, is so broad that it jeopardizes many of the rights that consumers have long enjoyed and that society has long benefited from. For example, as digitization and the science behind keeping those digits safe—encryption—becomes more important, researchers are increasingly stifled from freely discussing their ideas and distributing their tools over the Internet or elsewhere.

One example of how the DMCA is such a blunt instrument is the case of a multi-industry group called the Secure Digital Music Initiative (SDMI). In

September 2000, this group issued a public challenge to hackers and others to try to defeat the technology SDMI had invented to secure digital music. A team of researchers from Princeton and Rice Universities and Xerox Corporation took up the challenge and in short order overcame the protective "watermarks" that SDMI had devised. When the researchers tried to present their work at an academic conference, SDMI threatened the group, their employers, and the conference organizers with a lawsuit under the DMCA. The researchers withdrew their paper from the conference.

More chilling is the case of a Russian programmer named Dmitry Sklyarov. In July 2001, Sklyarov was jailed for several weeks and detained for five months in the United States after he spoke at a programming conference. Federal prosecutors were acting on a complaint from software maker Adobe, which alleged that Sklyarov and his employer, a Russian company called ElcomSoft, were developing and distributing over the Internet a program called Advanced e-Book Processor, which allowed owners of Adobe electronic books to convert them into Adobe Portable Document Format. The software allowed consumers who owned e-books to print these books by overcoming restrictions in the e-books' code. Sklyarov was not accused of infringing any copyrighted e-Book, nor of helping anybody to infringe. His alleged crime was working on a software tool that had many legitimate uses but also could have uses that could infringe copyrights. In the end, the Department of Justice permitted Sklyarov to return home, but still sued ElcomSoft under the DMCA. In December 2002 a jury acquitted ElcomSoft of all charges.

But the damage was done. The DMCA is so sweeping that it is reminiscent of a digital Taliban, inhibiting free speech and much commerce too. Books have been withdrawn and researchers have avoided working in or coming to the United States for fear of the DCMA.[3] Some point to the DMCA, which required that nascent Web radio stations pay royalties to record labels, as killing Web radio before it left the cradle, and ending what might have been, in time, a lucrative channel for music.[4]

THE LAW NEEDN'T BE AN ASS: A POSITIVE ROLE FOR LEGISLATION

Compared with radios and VCRs, digitization and the Internet represent a fundamentally different threat to the existing business models of copyright holders. New digital technologies combined with the Internet created much more significant threats. Audio compression technologies, such as the MP3 algorithm, condense audio tracks into a twelfth of their original digital space. A CD copied ("ripped") and converted into MP3 format could be sent over the Internet and downloaded onto someone's computer in minutes instead of hours. Over the past few years, millions of often perfect or near-perfect copies of copyrighted songs were available, for free, on various filesharing networks. By 2002, movies were starting to appear—illegally—on these networks, sometimes as soon as they were released to theaters. By 2003, some movies were available—again, illegally—on filesharing services *before* they had been released in theaters. One group of researchers from AT&T and the University of Pennsylvania laid the problem for this at the movie industry's doorstep.[5] Their findings indicated that much of the highest-quality pirated movies available for free on filesharing networks originated from industry insiders. As mentioned in Chapter 1, concern over this source of pirated movies led Jack Valenti, then head of the MPAA, to propose banning the MPAA membership from distributing copies of movies (sometimes sent before the film's official release) to members of the Academy of Motion Pictures Arts and Sciences, who vote on Academy Awards, as well as to movie critics. Still, those most immediately affected by piracy were the recording companies, which had suffered several years of declining sales, blaming online piracy for much of the slide. Although it was not at all clear how much piracy was at fault for the decline in sales, compared with, say, uninspired content, unimaginative business models, and poor management of technology (for example, not offering a legal alternative for several years even after Napster proved how popular such a service might be), Congress felt the recording industry's pain, and also shared the worries of the movie industry.

Prior to the rise of Napster, there had been a kind of détente between the recording industry and technology companies. In 1992, Congress passed the Audio Home Recording Act (AHRA), an amendment to the federal copyright law of 1976. Under the AHRA, all digital recording devices must incorporate a serial copy management system (SCMS). This system allows digital recorders to make a first-generation copy of a digitally recorded work, but does not allow a second-generation copy to be made from the first copy (users may still make as many first-generation copies as they want). The AHRA also provides for a royalty tax of up to $8 per new digital recording machine and 3 percent of the price of all digital audiotapes or discs. This tax is paid by the manufacturers of digital media devices and distributed to the copyright owners whose music is presumably being copied. In consideration of this tax, copyright owners agree to forever waive the right to claim copyright infringement against consumers using audio recording devices in their homes. This is commensurate with the fair use exception to copyright law, which allows consumers to make copies of copyrighted music for noncommercial purposes. The SCMS and royalty requirements apply only to digital audio recording devices. Because computers were not considered digital audio recording devices, they were not required to comply with the SCMS requirement.

Digital rights management (DRM) is a phrase used to describe a combination of software encryption and new hardware, designed to make digital copying impossible without permission. There are many DRM technologies currently available. In a practical sense, the variety of DRM systems is a problem because it is confusing to consumers who are never quite sure which DRM system is protecting the CD or DVD they purchase and how precisely they will be able to consume it. As additional DRM technologies emerge, this problem will likely become worse. (Consumer: "Can I play this DVD on my laptop?" Answer: "It depends; in what country did you buy the CD? What kind of processor powers your laptop? Which version of the DVD did you buy? . . .)

Critics of DRM contend that the technology, and the framework of the laws that would support DRM, could erode consumer rights enjoyed under concepts such as fair use and the doctrine of first sale. Private copying that is now legal, for listening to music or reading text on more than one device, for example, would also become subject to the permission of the record company or publisher. PC makers, among others, worried that many aspects of DRM could hobble the ability of PCs to play digital media.

By 2002, some large music labels began to produce CDs embedded with forms of DRM technology. These were copy-protection programs designed to prevent discs from being played on PCs. Sony has developed its own antipiracy technology, called key2audio, which prevents consumers from listening to CDs on any type of CD-ROM or DVD player. Sony announced in January 2002 that it had produced a total of ten million CDs for five hundred different albums that could not be played on personal computers due to its key2audio program. A second version of the software, key2audio4PC, permitted listeners to play copy-protected CDs on their personal computers. But the CDs were encrypted to limit usage to a single specific PC, preventing the user from playing them on alternative devices. BMG licensed antipiracy technology that prevented consumers from reformatting songs into MP3 files and burning copies, or making them available on filesharing systems. The software prevented listeners from playing the discs on CD-ROM drives and was also potentially damaging to amplifiers and speakers as well as having the ability to disable stand-alone CD burners.

The crux of the arguments of many DRM critics, that such technologies make products cost more and do less, was neatly captured in the matter of broadcast flags for high-definition digital broadcast television. In November 2003, the FCC ruled that digital TV tuners built after July 1, 2005, would need to include an antipiracy system called a broadcast flag, a DRM technology that is aimed at preventing the easy recording and dissemination (for example, via KaZaa) of high-definition television (HDTV) digital broadcasts. Broadcast flag technology embedded an invisible data tag—the broadcast flag—along with the picture and sound that is broadcast over the public airwaves. Consumers of broadcast HDTV would be able to record high-definition broadcasts but would not be able to share files (as they are currently able to do).

Luckily, in May 2005 a federal appeals court struck down the FCC's ruling, finding that the FCC did not have the authority to issue such a rule. But Congress can give the FCC the authority to do this.

The FCC's action was aimed at giving some protection to content owners who are concerned about the easy pirating of nearly perfect high-definition copies of their shows. This concern has led to the classic "start-up" or "chicken-and-egg" problem that has inhibited the expansion of HDTV: with content owners reluctant to allow their programming to be broadcast in HDTV, there has been little content available, which in turn has slowed sales of HDTV receivers, since there is little to watch in HDTV. This start-up problem is a problem for the government. They are encouraging HDTV because it uses less public air bandwidth than current analog broadcasts. When HDTV finally takes off, much of the public airwaves spectrum will become available. This is very valuable real estate that can be sold for other purposes, such as cell phone transmissions and the like.

In this case, it is only broadcasters who are in this mess. Cable and satellite networks do not use public airwaves, and they have different DRM mechanisms. Some worried that without some DRM protection for broadcasters, they could be at a serious disadvantage compared with cable and satellite competitors, if content owners such as producers of in-demand shows decide not to license or sell their shows to HDTV broadcasters for fear of piracy.[6]

But regardless whether the weapon is intellectual property or market power or some other tool, when industries allow themselves to enter the Fear stage, they usually lose the ability to coolly evaluate and deal with threats and complements.

FOR HOME USE ONLY:
THE BATTLE BETWEEN RADIO AND MUSIC

Initially, all programming produced and aired by NBC and CBS radio networks was live. Affiliates who chose to run the programming did so by broadcasting it from an AT&T phone line that transmitted the live performance. The programming was produced twice, once for audiences in the Eastern and Central time zones, and again for the Pacific time zone. These networks prohibited the use of recording other than for sound effects. However, recordings were soon to become more popular for radio broadcast. More and more programming was recorded, "transcribed" in the parlance of the day, on sixteen-inch discs, and broadcast by stations. Many stations dismissed the legions of studio musicians who had provided live music shows as well as atmospheric music for radio plays (and replaced some with a single musician on the versatile Hammond organ.)[7] At this time, many popular performers stamped their albums with the warning, "Not Licensed for Radio Broadcast."[8] They did not want to jeopardize exclusive performance contracts with networks. In a 1940 lawsuit, a court ruled that broadcasters could broadcast recordings they had purchased. The Supreme Court declined to review the case and, with this legal footing, the age of the disc jockey was born. Almost forty years after Fessenden's Christmas Eve broadcast, recorded music would occupy an ever-increasing proportion of broadcast time.

One stumble in this march came from a musicians' union, the American Federation of Musicians (AFM). Union president James C. Pertillo, with a unanimous vote of delegates at the union's 1942 convention, called a strike, halting all recording by union musicians. Petrillo pointed to the hundreds of radio stations that no longer employed musicians, victims of the Hammond organ and the disc jockey, and to films and jukeboxes that similarly left many musicians unemployed.[9] The union wanted employers of musicians to pay into a musician welfare fund. The recording companies objected. Within a year or two of the strike, most of the recording companies gave in, and the strike was called off.

Trouble with ASCAP

While musicians were being thrown out of radio work by records, the owners of the copyrights of recorded music were butting heads with broadcasters. Applications of existing law to new technologies often prove nettlesome. Then as now, the controversy centered on copyrights. The American Society of Composers, Authors and Publishers (ASCAP) was formed in 1914 to protect the copyright interests of the main content producers of the day—composers of popular music and show tunes—and their publishers. ASCAP eventually would seek to increase the fees it received from broadcasters to the point at which the networks organized to fight the threat and launched an organization to compete against ASCAP.

Some seek to interpret copyright laws liberally, applying them wholesale to new technologies. Others take a narrower view of the scope of copyright protection. Radio broadcast of music provoked serious challenges between broadcasters and copyright holders, and under the copyright laws that existed at the time, judges took a "half empty" view that leaned toward broadcasters at the potential expense of copyright owners. But long before these issues arose, another, less sophisticated technology had challenged copyright interpretation: player pianos.

In 1908 the White-Smith music publishing company sued the Apollo player piano company for infringing on its copyrights for two popular songs of the day, "Little Cotton Dolly" and "Kentucky Babe," by producing and selling piano rolls perforated to produce these tunes on player pianos. The Supreme Court took a surprisingly narrow view of copyright by finding that the perforations on a piano roll did not infringe on the titles. For the majority, Justice Day wrote, "After all, what is the perforated roll? The fact is clearly established in the testimony in this case that even those skilled in the making of these rolls are unable to read them as musical compositions."[10] The opinion observed "that in the year 1902 from seventy to seventy-five thousand of [player pianos] were in use in the United States and that from one million to one million and a half of such perforated musical rolls . . . were made in this country in that year. It is evident that the question involved in the use of such rolls is one of very considerable importance, involving large property interests and closely touching the rights of composers and music publishers."[11] In view of the popularity of the player pianos, the court wanted Congress to write a copyright law that would take into consideration the changing technologies and protect the property interests of many consumers who had already purchased player pianos.

The next year Congress did revisit the copyright issue and passed the Copyright Act of 1909. Under this law, copyright applied to mechanical reproduction and reproduction done publicly for profit. The new copyright law applied to phonograph records as well as player piano rolls. However, to guard against the development of music monopolies, the Copyright Act mandated that once a copyright owner issued a license for one form of mechanical reproduction, it was compelled to give the license to others, through the payment of a blanket copyright fee, then set at two cents per record.

Although the issue of mechanical rights and public and for-profit performances had been settled by the 1909 copyright act, some copyright holders, such as the popular composer Victor Herbert, seethed at the various uncompensated public performances of their copyrighted music occurring in dance halls and restaurants around the country. In early 1914, Herbert and his friend music lawyer Nathan Burkan, who had worked together on a friend-of-the-court brief in the White-Smith case, assembled a group of composers, including the famous Irving Berlin, and music publishers to form a performing rights society to make it easier to monitor public performances. The group named itself the American Society of Composers, Authors and Publishers and operated as a collection agent for its members. Proceeds were distributed among ASCAP members via a sliding scale based on the number of compositions owned. ASCAP had little success in selling licenses to allow the performance of ASCAP members' tunes to restaurants and dance halls. It looked to the courts to enforce its rights.

Soon after ASCAP was founded, it found its case. In that year, Herbert walked into Shanley's Restaurant, off Times Square in Manhattan, and heard his song "Sweethearts" being performed for patrons by musicians hired by the restaurant. Herbert sought an injunction against these kinds of public performances, which paid no royalties to copyright owners. A court ruled against Herbert, citing the fact that no money was charged for the performance. When a group of restaurant and hotel owners banded together to support Shanley's defense, Herbert and ASCAP were vitalized.[12] Herbert and his friends appealed the case to the United States Supreme Court. In 1917, the Supreme Court reversed the lower court's decision. In upholding the composer's claim, Oliver Wendell Holmes Jr. wrote the opinion for the majority: "If music did not pay, it would be given up. If it pays, it pays out of the public's pocket. Whether it pays or not, the purpose of employing it is profit, and that is enough."[13]

ASCAP expanded its fee-seeking efforts beyond theaters and dance halls to any place where performance for profit took place. Soon, there was no bigger consumer of ASCAP's music than radio.

In 1923, ASCAP looked to AT&T's radio broadcast station WEAF for a test case. ASCAP picked its target well. AT&T was a phone monopoly that enjoyed little public support and was famous for enforcing its own patents, having a history of using sharp elbows whenever it found itself in competition. AT&T paid up, purchasing a one-year license for $500 that allowed it to play all of the ASCAP-licensed music it wished to air. This arrangement became the industry standard.

In 1931, ASCAP claimed that the LaSalle Hotel in Kansas City, Missouri, violated its copyrights by playing songs broadcast on a radio show over speakers wired throughout the hotel. A court found that while the hotel could not legally perform the music without permission, it could project the music in the hotel if it were broadcast over the radio.[14] Under later revisions to copyright laws, and subsequent court opinions, such performances would be subject to royalty payments.

Broadcasters and ASCAP were complements. Working together, they could have benefited both radio and recorded music, ushering the technologies to Prosperity with publishers and composers collecting money along the way.

But ASCAP fell into a Fear mind-set, becoming a little greedy and shortsighted. In 1939, broadcasters paid ASCAP $4,300,000, or 67 percent of its entire annual income. While ASCAP depended upon radio for two-thirds of its income, radio broadcasters depended upon ASCAP for most of their content.[15] Throughout the 1930s ASCAP increased the license fees it charged for radio performances. Each ASCAP increase was met by protests from the radio broadcasters, who in the end usually gave in and agreed.

By 1939, broadcasters had begun to really chafe at the ASCAP increases. Sidney M. Kaye, a CBS attorney, designed an alternative rights management agency called Broadcast Music Incorporated (BMI). In effect, broadcasters set out to create their own complement. Under Kaye's plan, broadcasters contributed 50 percent of their 1937 ASCAP copyright payments to capitalize and fund the new organization. In exchange, participating broadcasters received non-dividend-paying shares in BMI.[16] It seems ASCAP did not fear competition from BMI. In spite of the entry of a new competitor, ASCAP announced a 100 percent rate increase for 1941 (which would amount to 5 to 10 percent of a station's advertising revenues).

By 1940, radio broadcasters had raised more than $1 million to fund BMI. Unwilling to pay ASCAP's rates, 650 broadcasters signed with BMI by the end of the year, with only two hundred re-signing with ASCAP.[17] While BMI did not have a large repertoire, it seemed to hint at the potential power of broadcasters to influence tastes by writing in a BMI pamphlet, "The public selects its favorites from the music which it hears and does not miss what it does not hear."[18] On January 1, 1941, the broadcasters' boycott of ASCAP began.

The upstart agency needed to build a catalog of music. BMI had little success in poaching ASCAP-affiliated artists. For a time, the stations that boycotted ASCAP had to rely on a handful of BMI tunes and songs with expired copyrights, such as Stephen Foster tunes. The music of most popular artists of the day, such as Irving Berlin, George Gershwin, Cole Porter, Rogers and Hart, and others were tied up in the ASCAP catalog. Similarly, much of the popular music from Europe was off limits to BMI because European rights agencies had reciprocal agreements with ASCAP. One exception was Latin American countries. Because ASCAP had overlooked this region, BMI was able to acquire many Latin tunes, and ASCAP-boycotting stations found themselves playing many sambas and rumbas in the early 1940s.

There had been earlier challenges to ASCAP. In 1924 the movie industry tried to supply silent movie houses with non-ASCAP music, but the effort failed. Some movie studios ended up buying music firms and joining ASCAP themselves. NBC and the industry group the National Association of Broadcasters (NAB) had tried to combat ASCAP in the early 1930s to no avail. In 1935 movie studio Warner Brothers, which had purchased a music firm, dropped out of ASCAP and tried to collect on its own. The studio controlled 20 percent of ASCAP's catalog and songs from star composers such as Noel Coward, George Gershwin, Jerome Kern, Cole Porter, and others. Still, radio stations preferred to deal with only one agency and dropped Warner Brothers music from their playlists. Warner Brothers was back in ASCAP within eight months.[19] This left ASCAP emboldened.

Where other attempts to supplant ASCAP failed, BMI was able to gain a foothold. By the 1950s, BMI reached parity with ASCAP in the number of tunes played over the radio. By 1999 BMI's rates had become very close to those assessed by ASCAP.

Aside from the merits of the positions of the broadcasters and ASCAP, the tension was exacerbated by a fundamental shift in the consumption of music in the country. Until radio became popular, songwriters sought any public performance of their work, in order to publicize the tunes and increase sales of sheet music, piano rolls, and phonographs. Although radio popularizes a tune, that popularity does not last as long. Radio was estimated to have shortened the life of a hit song from sixteen weeks in 1925 to just two to three months in 1940.[20] In 1927, a hit song may have sold two million copies of sheet music. After the advent of radio, a hit song sold less than 225,000 copies of sheet music.

Because of the technology shift provided by radio, overall sheet music sales declined. ASCAP looked for radio to make up the difference when the problem seemed to be created by a shift in technology without a concomitant shift in business model.

During the ASCAP "blackout," the group found that sales of their records and sheet music plummeted, from a rate of 300,000 copies sold per week to 120,000 copies sold per month.[21] In 1939, ASCAP-affiliated titles accounted for 100 percent of the top-selling sheet music in 1939. By 1941, that figure had fallen to just over 15 percent. Similarly, in 1940, ASCAP-affiliated songs accounted for 97 percent of the most-played titles on the radio. By 1941, ASCAP's share had fallen to zero.[22] After the blackout was resolved, ASCAP quickly regained its leadership but not before giving BMI a foothold. For example, while ASCAP ignored or otherwise shortchanged composers and performers of so-called "hillbilly" music (in other words, American folk or country) and "race" music (a phrase replaced in 1949 by "rhythm and blues," used to categorize styles of music such as blues, jazz, and gospel, then created and consumed mostly by black Americans), BMI courted artists in these genres.[23] While good for increased diversity in music, ASCAP's blackout accomplished nothing for the group and helped establish a competitor. Both ASCAP and BMI have since come under regulatory scrutiny by the federal government.

BIG SCREEN VERSUS SMALL: THE STUDIO SYSTEM JOINS TOGETHER AGAINST TELEVISION [24]

We saw at the beginning of this chapter how movie studios locked themselves in Fear at the prospect of the VCR in the 1970s. Interestingly, the studios had the same reaction twenty-five years earlier when they saw only a challenge and not a complement in television.

By the time the Paramount case was settled in 1949, the U.S. film industry had entered a prolonged downturn. During this period, movie attendance dropped by half, four thousand theaters closed, and studio profits fell dramatically. Studios also had to contend with what they perceived as a major technological challenge in the form of television. Although television had been demonstrated as early as the 1920s, its development was stalled during World War II, and regular commercial broadcasts had to wait until after the war. When the development of television networks continued in earnest, the studios saw only a new competitor. As noted in Chapter 3, in 1939 there were only around two hundred television sets in the United States, but by 1948 there were one million sets in the country, and that figure quadrupled by 1954.

By the late 1940s, movie studios had to absorb the impact of the deverticalization (spinning off of chains of theaters) imposed by the Paramount case. In addition, they reeled from the impacts of other forces, including shifting buyer needs characterized by a general dissatisfaction of audiences with the studio output at the time, migration of the movie-going population away from urban centers (and their theaters) to the growing suburbs, and a change in input costs that related to the disintegration of the contract system under which all actors and directors—stars and bit players alike—signed multiyear contracts with fixed wages in favor of profit-sharing contracts with actors and later directors. When television came on the horizon, studios saw only competition for eyeballs. In fact, studios prohibited their stars from appearing on television.

Movies Embrace Television for a While

Movie studios and television were not always competitors. In the early days of television, during World War II when its development was greatly slowed by the more pressing demands of the war effort, some movie studios saw television as a potential distribution channel for their products. Indeed, in the absence of the advertising model that eventually developed for broadcast television, some form of "home box office" was envisioned in order to make television financially feasible. A very interesting article from an issue in the wonderful, long-defunct magazine *The American Mercury* discussed the outlook for television. In an issue in July 1944, just a month after D-Day, a writer looked to a time when television would live up to the hype that had developed in the absence of the actual roll out. At that time, there were around ten thousand television sets receiving sporadic broadcasts from the nine stations in five cities in the United States.[25]

Comparing television to motion pictures seemed natural, and the probable economics of television seemed troublesome. E. F. MacDonald, the president of Zenith Radio Corporation, a maker of television sets before the superseding needs of the war forced it to switch to production of equipment vital to the war effort, described the problem: it cost movie studios more than $200,000 to produce even a B movie—an hour's entertainment—whereas the most expensive radio program at the time, the *Jack Benny Show,* cost less than $25,000 a week to produce. It seemed, to this TV set maker, that costs to support programming that could exploit the richness of the medium and meet the expectations of viewers who would have paid around $200 for a set (equivalent to over $2,000 in 2003) would exceed any advertiser's budget.[26]

MacDonald argued that the likely economics of television suggested three likely business models: theater television, in which television programming was transmitted to movie theaters; some kind of metering device attached to TV sets in the home; or wired television, "paid for as wired radio hookups like Muzak are by subscribers."[27] Everybody can now see how prescient MacDonald was about wired television; today about 60 percent of Americans are cable subscribers. But each model was tried, and one movie studio in particular, Paramount, was involved in several trials of different systems of pay television.

The idea of theater television had been tested on different occasions in the 1930s and then put on hold during World War II. After the war, the movie industry was interested in starting up the idea again, but was foiled by a combination of the FCC, which made few frequencies available for theater television, and the movie studios themselves, who failed to agree on standards and the aftermath of antitrust actions that separated studios from chains of theaters, at a time when tighter vertical integration might have overcome some of the standardization issues.

Metered television had been tried too. For a time, Paramount was an investor in the ill-starred DuMont Television Company, which manufactured TV sets and established a network. The studio was also a controlling investor in a company called Scophony Corporation of America, which had patented a signal-scrambling process consisting of a few extra vacuum tubes in a TV set. Scophony believed that broadcasters could broadcast a scrambled signal that could be descrambled by subscribers with these special sets using a celluloid "key card" that could be purchased every week or so. At say, ten cents a week, an audience of three million (top radio shows attracted thirty million listeners each week) could support programming that would, in theory anyway, cost them forty cents to view in a theater. Alas, in 1945 antitrust actions brought an end to Paramount's investment in Scophony.

Less elegant was the idea of a coin box in the home. I remember as a kid staying in a boarding house in England in the 1970s that had a coin box to operate hot water. A hot bath is one thing, but television is a necessity. The inconvenience of this system must have been staggering. Still, the idea was tested in Palm Springs, California, in the early 1950s, again by Paramount. This system, called telemeter, used scrambled television signals sent over telephone lines. When customers deposited the correct amount of change in the coin box, the telemeter descrambled the signal. The system debuted in 1953, showing a USC-Notre Dame football game (presaging the popular college sports packages now available on satellite TV services) for $1.00 and a first-run Paramount movie, *Forever Female,* for an additional $1.35. Paramount stopped the test in 1955, fearing additional antitrust action from the government.[28]

Perhaps mindful of the antitrust actions they had suffered twice in the past twenty years, movie studios did not resume efforts to coopt the nascent television industry. Still, TV was biting into the studios' revenue. As early as 1951, movie attendance was dropping sharply in cities with TV broadcast stations, and a wave of theatre closings spread across the country.[29]

Among the colorful moguls that populate the history of movie and television production, one in particular, former talent agent and latter-day studio head Lew Wasserman, had an enormous impact on the structure of the movie and television industries. Wasserman helped break the contract system that had been a key feature of the vertically integrated studio system, and bought what had been a second-rate studio (Universal) when long-time veteran studio heads feared television and despaired for their futures. Wasserman did not despair for Hollywood in the face of television. He recalled in an interview in 1966, "Every new medium has brought predictions of the death of every other. Radio was said to be all washed up, but stations are selling for higher prices than ever. When television came along, the studios were prepared to sell all their product, fire their people, and fold up. But we're only at the beginning of the beginning."[30]

THE BOSTON STRANGLER? MOVIE STUDIOS AND TELEVISION FEAR THE VCR

In 1976, a group of movie studios, led by Universal Studios, sued Sony Corporation, maker of the Betamax video recorder. To the studios, the VCR represented a technology whose main purpose was to violate copyrights. An appeals court found in favor of the studios, and the case went to the Supreme Court, which in a 5 to 4 decision narrowly reversed the appeals court ruling and found that the ability of VCRs to record broadcast television for private viewing at a more convenient time (this practice was called "time shifting") represented a legitimate use for the technology. At the time of the ruling, Jack Valenti, the chairman of the MPAA, was quoted as saying, "The VCR is to the American film producer and the American public as the Boston strangler is to a woman home alone."[31]

Sony introduced its Betamax video tape recorder to the U.S. consumer market in 1975. In that year, Sony produced 20,000 units. In 1976, Sony produced 175,000 Betamax units, while competitors introduced VHS-format VCRs, incompatible with Betamax, producing 110,000 units in the same year.[32] Soon after, the technology was catapulted into the Ascension stage as millions of VCRs were purchased by consumers.

Sony promoted the VCR's ability to "time shift" programming, meaning the VCR gave consumers the ability to record a television program broadcast over the air even while watching another show on a different channel, something remarkable for consumers at the time.

Time shifting provided sufficient motivation for consumers to purchase VCRs, whether in the Betamax or VHS format, and sales increased rapidly. Worried about their ability to control their copyrighted material once it had been taped by consumers, Universal, Disney, and other studios filed suit against Sony in 1976, claiming that its Betamax VCR, and the home taping it allowed, constituted contributory copyright infringement. Sony drew analogies between home audiotaping introduced in the 1960s, a practice not tested in the courts but nonetheless widely accepted, and home videotaping. Universal had a possible dual motivation in that it may have wanted to prevent Betamax from capturing a significant segment of the fledgling home video market before its parent company, MCA (Music Corporation of America), could introduce its own competing home video technology.

The initial ruling of the lower court in favor of Sony hung on the court's interpretation of the fair use doctrine as it pertained to consumers. Addressing the matter of retailing of videocassettes, the court let stand the First Sale Doctrine of the 1976 Copyright Act, which stated that the first purchaser of a copyrighted work (such as a motion picture on videocassette) could use it in any way the purchaser saw fit as long as copyright was not violated by illegal duplication, and so on. This right extended to the rental of videocassettes purchased from Hollywood studios. Prior to the arrival of the VCR, film studios received a portion of the box office, that is, a fee each time one of their films was shown. The court's interpretation of the First Sale Doctrine threatened to undermine Hollywood's control over the use of its product.

Losing on appeal, Sony took the case to the United States Supreme Court, which very nearly voted to deny certiorari—not hear the case—in which event the appeals court decision would have stood. In the end, the court did hear the case and voted 5 to 4 to reverse in January 1984. In the close case Sony had help from many quarters, including the long-time children's television personality Mister Rogers. As Justice Stevens noted in his majority opinion, Fred Rogers of *Mister Rogers' Neighborhood* deserved "specific mention" in that he had "absolutely no objection to home taping for noncommercial use and expressed the opinion that it is a real service to families to be able to record children's programs and to show them at appropriate times."[33]

REFUSING TO FACE THE MUSIC: DISRUPTING THE RECORD COMPANIES

For the past ten years, the recording industry has been the poster child for industries in the Fear stage. Since the late 1990s, the industry has been in a panic. As Lord Byron did not say, much about the threats and opportunities of digitization, dark and light, meet in the aspect of the current music industry. The industry has tread fearfully into new technology over the past few years and has many problems to show for its trepidation. Sales of recorded music have declined globally and in the United States for each of the past three years. According to the Recording Industry Association of America (RIAA), recorded music sales declined 31 percent between mid-2000 and mid-2003. And it did not look like the trend was getting better. The head of the RIAA put the blame on filesharing, saying "This is not a victimless crime; people are really suffering from the impact of peer-to-peer downloading."[34]

The RIAA had earned itself tremendous consumer ill will with its much publicized decision to sue individuals who shared "even one song" over the Internet through the popular filesharing sites such as Napster and KaZaa. Some studios took a different route: the day after the RIAA announced its disastrous sales figures in its mid-year report, the leading music label, Universal Music Group, announced that it was slashing prices of its CDs and encouraging resellers to drop their prices to below $10 per CD.

The fidelity of the songs found on filesharing services was not always high, and files were often mislabeled, on accident or due to the spurious intent of the person posting the files. Still, for millions of users, the files offered by Napster and its successors such as KaZaa were good enough. And that was an important point. For many years, the record company's stock in trade had been the CD, and before that the long-playing album (LP). The quality of the sound recording was the highest available, but the record company selected the titles to be bundled on the product and priced it—most recently, at about $15–$17 per CD. Often, buyers were faced with buying a CD of ten or twelve tracks when they only wanted a few.

When digital technologies (such as CDs) and increased processing power and memory (along with CD rippers and burners for copying CDs) met the new codecs (compression technologies such as MP3) and high-bandwidth networking (such as PCs connected to the Internet via high-speed lines in dormitories and homes) millions of *good enough* music files were swapped. This became a disruptive technology for the record companies. The concept of disruptive technologies was pioneered in the mid-1990s by Harvard Business School professor Clayton M. Christensen. In his book *Innovator's Dilemma,* Christensen describes how disruptive technologies appear to offer lower quality or performance—in the case of music filesharing, imperfect or frequently mislabled MP3 files, played over tinny computer speakers, compared with store-bought CDs played over a proper stereo.[35] According to Christensen, victims of disruptive technologies find that the lower-quality technology is good enough for many users and eats into the market of conventional producers, in this case, the record companies.

The flip side to disruptive technologies, as described by Christensen, is the "overshoot" of incumbent players. The producers of the highest-quality products tend to continue to develop their products, satisfying the demands of the most advanced customers and, in the process, outstripping or over-shooting the needs of the majority of the market. This leaves producers making products with features that most customers do not want and will not pay for. (This is the eponymous "innovator's dilemma" from which the book takes its title.) In terms of the music industry, CDs tend to overshoot most of the market, which would seem to prefer to obtain just a few tracks off of any given CD. It was not until 2002 (three years after the initial disruption represented by Napster) that many record companies began to offer tracks online. The delay was due to the fact that the record companies did not know how to make a profit in this new marketplace, or how to control their content once it was released in digital format. Indeed, Apple's Steve Jobs, coming from the computer industry, took the recording industry by the hand to a channel (iTunes) that offered the industry some profits from online distribution.

How did the Napster phenomenon take hold? In the span of eleven months, Napster went from an obscure computer program to public enemy number one for record companies. That is fast, even by so-called Internet time, whereby things get sped up. Napster arrived at the confluence of several events. By 1999, computers were in millions of homes (and dorms), these computers were networked to the Internet, and navigation of the Internet was made easy by the World Wide Web and by Web browsers such as Netscape Navigator and Microsoft's Explorer. All of this was true in 1997, to a lesser but still sufficient degree. What was different between 1997 and 1999 was MP3 technology. Essentially an agreed-upon algorithm or formula for compressing digital data into more manageable sizes, MP3 files were sufficiently popular in 1999 that millions of users could be attracted to a software program that could be cheaply distributed over the Internet. Whereas AOL had spent millions of dollars littering the country with CDs only a few years earlier, Napster did essentially the same thing, almost without cost. It seems the old maxim is true: build a better mousetrap and the world will beat a path to your door—providing the technological forces are aligned. In the case of filesharing, the necessary forces -the PCs on every desktop, easy networking (the Internet and WWW with browsers), and finally MP3 compression standards—came into alignment in 1999, and the recording companies have been battling them ever since.

As of early 2003, the global market for recorded music, valued at roughly $33.7 billion, was dominated by five major players: Universal Music Group (UMG), Sony, Warner Music Group (WMG), EMI, and BMG. These "big five" together accounted for roughly 74 percent of the industry in 2002. UMG led the big five, with 23 percent of the market. This oligopoly structure was the result of several years of consolidation, motivated by the desire to create synergies from combining record company assets, from production to distribution, under one roof in order to better compete globally.

By the first half of 2002, world sales of recorded music had fallen by 9.2 percent in dollar value, and unit shipments were down 11.2 percent.[36] In 2002, the worldwide recording industry suffered its third straight year of declining sales. Sony told investors it expected music revenues to fall an additional 13–15 percent in 2003. In the United States, sales had also declined steadily over the previous three years, with sales of recorded music falling 8.2 percent in dollar value and 11.2 percent in unit shipments.[37] During the same 2002 period, the RIAA reported that seizures for counterfeit CDs had risen by 69.9 percent. CD drives that could record (burn) as well as play CDs were standard issue on even the most inexpensive PCs, enabling millions of consumers to potentially bypass bootlegging middlemen and duplicate their own CDs.

The major recording labels and their industry associations blamed piracy for an estimated $5 billion loss in 2002. MP3 fileswapping via P-to-P services such as KaZaa and others was still rampant despite the much publicized legal action that shut down Napster. According to CNet's Download.com, over 211 million copies of KaZaa's P-to-P software had been downloaded as of April 2003, growing by an estimated 3 million per week. Even though this number included upgrades and multiple copies downloaded by individual users, the figure dwarfed the estimated 70 million copies downloaded by the Napster community. The recording industry feared that the precedent—or worse, tradition—of free downloadable music had been established for some consumers.

The industry also worried about fast-changing information-processing technologies, such as increasingly powerful processors, CD burners on PCs, and consumer broadband Internet connectivity. Consumers could now make perfect digital copies of recordings and trade them around the world effortlessly. With a broadband connection, it took only a few minutes to download MP3 files and burn them onto a CD or pass them on to others. Information processing advances continued to outpace not only the music industry's attempts to safeguard content, but also its attempts to find a business model that still allowed consumers many of the fair use activities of the past, such as the ability to transfer songs onto portable devices.

Further, these recording heavyweights—all except EMI, which, at this writing, is still an independent music company with assets relating only to recorded music—were nestled into highly diversified portfolios of companies. For example, industry market share leader UMG belonged to the troubled media conglomerate, Vivendi Universal (now known as Vivendi S.A.). In 2002, UMG represented 22 percent of total Vivendi revenues. The other major labels represented smaller portions of their parent company's total revenues and were often dwarfed by other business units. The big five record labels that were owned by media conglomerates had been referred to as mere "duchies in large media empires with other, often conflicting priorities." Indeed, Sony Electronics represented a whopping 70 percent of Sony Corporation's total revenues while Sony Music represented only 8 percent. Similarly, AOL Time Warner was refocusing on high-speed Internet services (one common use of which is downloading free music), much to the reputed distaste of its Warner Music subsidiary. Elsewhere, two main music executives at BMG resigned in outrage at parent company Bertelsmann's investment in Napster.

While piracy was a major concern for the labels, and the economic downturn in the United States may have added to the industry's headaches, some industry executives looked for problems within the industry itself. The music industry in general was saddled with the problem of redeeming itself in the eyes of consumers, who seemingly harbored disgust for the sustained high level of CD prices and often characterized the industry as greedy. Howard Stringer, chairman and CEO of Sony Corporation of America, was quoted as saying, "In the music business, the problem is easy to see. We alienated music people; we alienated the consumer when we cranked up CD prices too high, and we alienated retailers for the same reason. There was dissatisfaction at the number of tracks on a CD that were any good. We upset the artists because they felt they were being ripped off. And device manufacturers were confused about it all."[38]

We'll See You in Court

The RIAA handled many of the industry's important lawsuits, including current cases targeting all of the filesharing services such as KaZaa and Morpheus. It was the RIAA's lawsuit that resulted in the shutdown of Napster. Hilary Rosen, chairman and CEO of the RIAA, commented on her group's litigation against the P-to-P networks: "We knew we were losing the PR battle. It was a tsunami. But instinctively, I always thought that people thought we were right. They thought it was a free ride, and boy was it fun, but it would never last. So while I knew [the labels'] political strategy was drawing blood, I knew we'd win."[39]

It was the RIAA that filed the 2003 lawsuit against Verizon described earlier. In addition to handling most of the lawsuits related to piracy, the RIAA undertook an aggressive education campaign. With evidence that many users conducted their downloading from their office or university-owned lines, the RIAA warned companies and schools about copyright infringements taking place with their hardware and networks. In March 2003, the RIAA sent three hundred letters to companies, warning "In short, your computer network and resources are being used to illegally distribute copyrighted music on the

Internet. . . . We strongly urge you to take immediate steps to prevent the continued infringement of our members' sound recordings on your corporate network. These acts of infringement could expose your employees and your company to significant legal damages."

The RIAA has also encouraged labels to ease licensing restrictions, develop digital copy protections for music, and invest more in online subscription services, focusing on the long-term potential instead of short-term losses. Rosen also proposed a levy paid by ISPs to labels for allowing consumers free access to filesharing services. In her keynote speech, Rosen said, "Let's face it. They [the ISPs] know there's a lot of demand for broadband simply because of the availability [of file sharing]."[40]

CONCLUSION

It is in the nature of incumbent companies and established industries to be conservative because they usually have something to conserve. The prospect of change often puts companies and industries in the Fear mind-set, in which they see new complements only as competitors and fail to make the leap to envision new outlets for future Prosperity. Incumbents have long-established ways of doing business that generate revenues. Managers are likely to warily view technologies that threaten to alter their established ways of doing business, especially if it is not clear immediately how the incumbents can make money from them. And this is almost always the case with new technologies; because they are new, there are not preestablished ways for incumbents to make money.

Economic distress compounds the problem. As we saw, ASCAP faced declining sheet music sales and tried to bleed dry radio broadcasters and movie studios to make up the difference. However, its Fear response eventually generated a competitor in BMI. Movie studios faced declining attendance at the same time that television started to become a force, which disposed studios to seeing television as yet another threat to deal with rather than a potentially lucrative distribution channel. Similarly, the recording industry's golden goose represented by CDs was finally tiring out when another aspect of digitization (P-to-P and online distribution) appeared and locked the industry into the Fear stage, from which it still has not completely recovered.

5 PROSPERITY

W HEN THE MOVIE STUDIOS REALIZED the power of television as a distribution channel for films, they set out selling their vast libraries of content for television exhibition. By 1953, during the first Academy Award ceremony to be televised, emcee Bob Hope was able to quip, "Television—that's where movies go when they die."[1] It was a very profitable burying place. By 1960, some studios made almost half of their annual revenue from television.

Similarly, movie studios soon learned that VCRs were gold mines for them. By 1998 movie studios made half of their annual revenue from movie rentals and sales. That percentage has been increasing every year since.

To get to Prosperity with a new technology, movie studios had to think a little bit differently about their businesses and their relationships with customers. As we have seen, both television and the VCR weakened the roles of exhibitors in the movie industry value chain. Technology thrust upon movie studios new value chains in the form of new distribution channels: first TV and VCRs and later Internet-based channels.

Today, television networks face a similar threat and opportunity with upstart companies such as YouTube, the Internet startup company acquired by Google in 2006 that attracts millions of viewers to videos posted on its site. In the space of a few months, broadcaster NBC went from making YouTube remove *Saturday Night Live* clips to doing an advertising deal with the company.

NBC seems to be catching on to the requirement for Prosperity; it was thinking differently about itself and its business.

How is it that an industry changes its point of view—begins to think differently about itself—and sees what it had feared was a competitor as a complement? It is difficult to say when enlightened self-interest that leads to Prosperity overcomes Fear. By the time the legal niceties are worked out, it is usually too late. Take the case of video tape rentals. When the industry was born, nobody was sure whether the practice of renting a video was legal. But since the studios were clearly making money from the rental industry, they were able to be thrust into Prosperity. (The idea for renting videos came from entrepreneurs outside of the studios.)

This is only somewhat different from the situation the recording industry faced with Napster and its cousins. Napster's technology demonstrated the ability to efficiently deliver music over the Internet, and its popularity proved the appetite from consumers for this ability. For a long time, the recording industry saw only the copyright infringement and missed the huge opportunity for itself that underlay the infringement. The recording industry was right to fear filesharing as practiced by Napster, but it was not right to demonize the practice. For several years after the genie was so publicly out of its bottle, the recording industry made no real attempts to capitalize from the forces that enabled Napster to become so popular. The biggest difference with the video rental example is that nobody took the recording industry by the hand and led it to a new Prosperity stage. Even allowing for hindsight, the recording industry should have seen for itself how easy it would be for them to offer a legal alternative. Two obstacles stood in the way: desire to protect its comfortable business model of selling music on CDs and the unwillingness of recording companies to cooperate with each other to license music for online distribution. Given that the recording industry is somewhat concentrated, this should have been not too difficult. But no major studio was willing to jeopardize the CD business model—until Apple's Steve Jobs showed them the way with iTunes. The recording industry left it to a computer company to dictate the cost and terms of what is becoming a very compelling distribution channel. Still, as you will see, things may be looking up, especially for more enlightened recording companies like Universal.

Motion picture companies felt, with some justification, that they would be the next to experience the sharp ends of the forces that so hurt their cousins in the recording industry. They may be right, but there are important differences between the two industries. One big difference is in the usage models that govern how consumers consume records and movies. For most of the past century, consumers have wanted to own music, even if it was only on paper (that is, sheet music). The same was not true for movies. Of course, even though skeptics who doubted that consumers would actually want to own copies of movies and watch them over and over again were proven dramatically wrong, music is still far more fungible than movies. Music was particularly vulnerable to the forces we are discussing, and, absent a coherent industry-wide response, the recording industry has been taken to the brink of irreversible change. Music could end up becoming a loss leader for consumer electronics companies or retailers, or a tool to increase sales of iPods and bring in shoppers to Wal-Mart's Website—in short, a commodity where it once had been a premium product generating premium profits.

The movie industry seems to believe that it benefits from the slow rollout of consumer broadband, computers that are still not powerful enough to give a good movie-watching experience, and the fact that consumers and technology companies still have not worked out the home office-living room barrier. It is not fun to watch a movie on your computer while sitting at your desk, or even while reclining holding your laptop computer on your belly. However, this is a perfectly acceptable way for many consumers to enjoy music.

For now, the movie industry has mostly benefited by digitization, and its apparent killer app, the DVD player. The explosive growth in consumer adoption of DVD players has presented the movie industry enormous profits, but some challenges. The profits come from DVD sales. Take the movie *Finding Nemo:* in the six months that the film was in theatrical release, before it was legally available on DVD or video, the movie took in $340 million at the box office. Pixar, its creator, and Disney, its distributor, netted a little less than half of that amount, with the balance going to exhibitors. (This was before Disney's acquisition of Pixar.) However, after two months of its release on DVD and video, the movie sold twenty-seven million copies (most on DVD) and earned Pixar and Disney $459 million, a windfall they did not have to share with theater owners.[2]

This boon, though, has upset the long-established and comfortable business practices of studios. There are set windows for the release of films into their various distribution channels. First, movies are released into domestic theaters, then undergo foreign theatrical release; next they are sold to the video rental market and then the home video market (remember studios tried to ban these channels), and then onto the pay-per-view market, followed by movie channels and finally broadcast TV. This cycle can take as long as two years to complete. Digitization has upset this routine. The consumer demand for DVDs, plus the threat of piracy made easier with digitization and Internet distribution, is compressing the various release windows for films. Upsetting the cycle and using new technologies to serve consumers in new ways is usually the ticket to Prosperity, but studios will have to change their business models to do so.

Although movies may get a temporary reprieve from having their business models forcibly changed by technology, the television industry will not be so lucky. In particular, the broadcast television industry (for 40 percent of Americans this is the only form of television they get) is right now facing fundamental challenges to the way it does business. The home office-living room balance is quickly being shifted in favor of the living room by set-top boxes that are becoming increasingly powerful. They look more like computers and have big storage capacities. Services such as Tivo and others allow users to record countless hours of programming and even email shows to their friends, or, with a little more ingenuity, post them to peer-to-peer distribution networks such as KaZaa. Not to be left out, cable companies are beginning to offer the same types of services as Tivo along with new set-top boxes that give consumers more options than ever, but also put at risk the basic business model of broadcast television networks who rely on providing advertisers a specific audience demographic.

In the broadcast television industry, there is talk about going back to the future, by relying more on product placements and whole-show sponsorships, like they used to do in the 1950s. This is risky, however, as the industry seems to have lost its touch with such programs. The latest examples have been flops, and even former film and television mogul (now Internet mogul) Barry Diller, for all of his demonstrated success picking programming, was not able to get the concept off the ground even though that was an express goal of his when he owned at the same time e-commerce assets, television, and movie-production studios. (Diller had hoped to sell items featured on his programming through his e-commerce channels; for example, "buy the jewelry, skirt, or lamp featured on tonight's program by dialing or surfing the Home Shopping Network.")

Perhaps the only thing that is clear about the impact of these forces on content industries is that what it takes to succeed is going to be different in the future. Good (that is, in demand) content will always be necessary, but it will not be sufficient. Companies will need to understand technology too and understand how best to apply it to their businesses. Disney seems to believe this now. As late as 2005, news reports carried stories about how Disney was requiring its traditional animators to learn more about computers and computer-generated (CG) animation, in large part because Disney's traditional animation features have fared poorly at the box office compared with the CG animation features produced by Disney's (then) partner Pixar and others. This reveals a conundrum for the company (and other content producers): if CG and regular animation films cost the same to produce, which seems to be true, what explains the difference in box office receipts lately? Why should Disney expect that a CG animation film will perform better than a regular animation film if they both are made by the same teams that brought us *Treasure Island*? For Disney, was the problem the stories or the mode of animation or some combination of the two? In purchasing Pixar and putting the company's cofounder and creative director John Lasseter in charge of the Magic Kingdom's animation, Disney seems to be trying to grapple with the new technology and perhaps (time will tell) more fully embracing Pixar, which had been set to shift from a complement (Disney distributed its films) to a big competitor.

GOLD RECORDS: THE GOLDEN AGE OF RADIO— FOR RECORDING COMPANIES

For a long time, radio was the primary conduit for exposure of records and popular songs to the public. It also became a fountain of royalties for artists. In 1953, ASCAP members received payments on the basis of nineteen million performances for writers, who received 8 cents per airplay, and sixteen million performances for publishers, who received 24 cents. A song that was heard mostly through recordings generated an average of $6,000 worth of earnings to its writer and publisher, compared with $15,000 generated on average through songs that had radio and television airplay. Of course, sheet music sales were drying up. Hits sold around 10,000–15,000 sheet copies in the advent of radio and TV, whereas a popular song used to sell three quarters of a million copies.[3] Radio and television became such important outlets for exposing songs to the public that the abuse of the power of these mediums in this regard spawned a new word—payola—in which programming managers and disc jockeys were paid by record promoters to play specific records.

Within the span of forty years, the recorded music business in the United States alone grew from $100 million to $6 billion, much of this due to the draw from radio.

Brief tempests about payola aside, the gravity generated by radio (and later television too) pulled records off the shelves. The recording industry has always been an up-and-down business, with a few years of plenty punctuating years of lean. Like so much else in entertainment, it is a hit business. At midcentury, when the power of radio was at its peak and television was coming on as a force, record sales hit an all-time high. In the late 1950s, the recording industry's annual sales exceeded $500 million for the first time, largely thanks to the demand spurred by radio. As rock and roll music emerged in the mid-1950s, the industry found a new "killer app." Still, it was a tough business, with only one out of every thirty releases a hit. It took sales of forty thousand records to recoup a record's production costs.[4]

The industry started with high concentration, with RCA and Columbia accounting for most of the industry's sales. By the middle of the twentieth century, four labels dominated the industry. After a brief spell of success for independent labels, which introduced genres of music such as rock and roll and rhythm and blues, which had been ignored by the established labels, the familiar oligopoly structure reemerged. Technology, in the form of high-fidelity stereo records, helped spur the recording industry to ever-increasing sales. By the late 1970s, record sales approached $4 billion a year. With the advent of cassette tapes and then CDs, the industry was bringing in $40 billion worldwide annually from retail sales by 1998—before the current malaise set in.

TELEVISION SAVES THE STUDIOS

Beginning in 1947, the movie industry entered a ten-year recession, not unlike today's hard times for the recording industry, in which attendance dropped by half and four thousand theaters went out of business. Naturally, they blamed television for their problems. But the Hollywood downturn had more to do with migration to the suburbs, away from city centers, and a postwar baby boom along with a related increase in appliance purchases, including radios, which enjoyed a boom as Hollywood was suffering.[5] At the time of this turmoil, a famous and successful producer predicted, "Hollywood is like Egypt, full of crumbling pyramids. It'll never come back. It'll just keep on crumbling until finally the wind blows the last studio prop across the sands."[6]

After the studios abandoned their attempts to directly enter the television industry, it still did not occur to them that TV could represent a good distribution channel. The struggling medium did not look as if its then-paltry advertising revenues could support the prices studios wanted to charge to show their films on the small screen. As television took off in the late 1940s, the picture for the studios brightened.

Live television programming was more expensive to produce than movies were to rent for broadcast exhibition. Studios first released their pre-1948 films; newer movies were subject to Screen Actors Guild (SAG) and Writers Guild of America residual compensation schemes, which increased their costs to TV broadcasters. Within three years, studios earned over $220 million on 3,700 films sold or leased to television. The average price per feature rose from $10,000 to $75,000.[7] Because these films had been fully amortized, this represented pure profit to the ailing studios.

The next step would be to get directly involved (again) in the new medium. It took a Hollywood titan and a future president of the United States to accomplish this. Lew Wasserman, the head of Hollywood talent agency MCA, and a client of his, an actor on the decline in Hollywood named Ronald Reagan, helped change the way Hollywood viewed television.

Production of live television tended to be concentrated in New York, and its performers were represented by the American Federation of Television and Radio Artists (AFTRA) union. Prerecorded television tended to be concentrated in Los Angeles, and its actors were represented by SAG. SAG had long-standing rules against its members appearing in movies produced by talent agencies, due to the conflict of interest inherent when talent agencies hired their own clients. However, the union had not yet established comparable restrictions for television, which was just then picking up steam. MCA sought a formal waiver from any union rules prohibiting joint agency-production ownership in television in order to grow its television production company, Revue, into a major production studio for recorded television while maintaining its successful agency business.

In July 1952, MCA persuaded the chairman of the guild, its client, actor Ronald Reagan, to propose to the SAG board that it grant a waiver allowing MCA (and only MCA) to produce prerecorded television shows while maintaining its agency business. In the midst of the downturn that hit Hollywood at the time, the board, made up of actors who had a lot less work than they had had earlier in the 1940s, and fearful of the downward pressure on salaries experienced by performers in live television (who were represented by the competing union) voted to grant MCA the waiver. This waiver and Wasserman's foresight enabled MCA to expand from its base as the dominant talent agency to become, by 1960, the world's biggest producer and distributor of television content.

Wasserman's belief in the value of television to the movie industry spurred MCA's next step toward becoming an entertainment powerhouse. In 1957, MCA purchased the library of Paramount's films made prior to the decree in 1948, in a deal valued at $50 million. At the time, it was considered a good deal for Paramount, as other studios (who were similarly still hurting from the impact of the sales of their theaters forced by the Paramount decree) such as RKO and Warner Brothers, had sold their pre-1948 libraries for much less. With the coming of television's appetite for old movies, MCA would realize an estimated $1 billion on the deal.[8]

Even though he was bullish on television, Wasserman did not believe movie studios would be overtaken by the desert any time soon. In 1959, MCA purchased Decca Records, which controlled Universal Pictures Company. The deal cost MCA only $11.25 million, but its overhead structure totaled $7.5 million per year.[9] This meant that MCA had to churn out content at a pace similar to studios in the days when they could force their B pictures down the throats of helpless theatergoers. With his agency business, television production arm, Paramount film library, and now Universal Pictures studio, Wasserman had assembled an entertainment juggernaut from assets that many thought had no future. Wasserman, however, set out not only to buy, but also to build these assets into something new. He recalled later, "Very few companies in the industry had spent money on capital improvement programs. The theory had been, don't spend any money you can't charge off to a film. I'm not going to say we can walk on water, but we were defying conventional thinking."[10] By "defying conventional thinking," Wasserman helped change the way the movie industry thought about television and helped the studios find new avenues of distribution for their films.

Although the government eventually forced the divorce of talent agencies and production interests, Hollywood by then had been convinced of the usefulness of television. As color television came out in the 1960s, studios began releasing post-1948 films. Networks began programming the newer movies in primetime, whereas old films had been relegated to the non-prime hours. The leasing revenue earned by studios when television networks broadcast their movies increased throughout the 1960s. Films typically earned around $150,000 per showing from television networks in the early 1960s, increasing to around $400,000 by the middle of the decade. In 1967, networks paid Hollywood studios $270 million for movies, and by the following year, networks were paying $800,000 to broadcast newer films (although by no means were these recent releases).[11]

VIDEOS AND VCRS: A CASH MACHINE FOR STUDIOS

At the time that VCRs were first being purchased for home use, it had not occurred to movie studios to capture this channel themselves. Studios, which had initially overlooked and then fought the lucrative distribution channel represented by television less than twenty-five years earlier, left it to others to come up with another new distribution channel for film. Instead this market first fell to a video-equipment entrepreneur named Andre Blay in Farmington Hills, Michigan. The story is well told in *Fast Forward*, a book by *New Yorker* writer James Lardner. When VCR tapes reached two hours in length, Blay realized there was a potential market for movies prerecorded on tape. In the fall of 1976, Blay wrote a "cold call letter" to the chief executive officers of every Hollywood studio, save one, Universal (which was then in the middle of a protracted lawsuit against Sony over its VCR), asking for the rights to sell their movies on video tape. Only MGM and Fox responded. MGM said it was considering the market for itself and declined to sell to Blay. In July 1977, Fox, which was also testing the market, agreed to sell Blay the rights to movies that had already been sold to broadcast television and were at least four years old. The Fox deal called for an advance of $300,000, plus a minimum of $500,000 a year against a royalty of $7.50 on each tape sold. Blay took out a bank loan for about one and a half million dollars, but he got started, selling copies of *Butch Cassidy and the Sundance Kid, M*A*S*H, Patton, The French Connection,* and others, fifty titles in all.[12] He formed his company, Magnetic Video, and was off.

Unsure where to sell his tapes, Blay explored various channels such as appliance retailers, and spent $65,000 on an ad in *TV Guide* announcing his Video Club of America. Though he sold his fifty titles for $50 each, customers beat a path to his maildrop. Blay had to keep his prerecorded video tape production facility (also a first) going twenty-four hours a day, producing twenty thousand Beta and VHS tapes a month. By the end of 1978, Blay had sold 250,000 cassettes.[13]

With videos selling for $50 apiece, the next logical step was video rental. It fell to another businessman, Los Angeles entrepreneur and erstwhile struggling actor George Atkinson, to develop this concept. Atkinson was running a super-8 projector and film rental business. His customers would pay $25 to rent a projector, screen, and old movie for an evening. When Atkinson read in the papers about Blay's deal with Fox, the concept of renting videos dawned on him. To test his idea, Atkinson ran an ad in the *Los Angeles Times* stating "Video for Rent" that invited customers to fill in and return a coupon with their choice of video. Of course, Atkinson had no stock, but his research yielded "about a thousand coupons" in less than a week. With seed capital of $10,000 from a high school friend, Atkinson bought Blay's videos from a distributor for $3 above wholesale, unable to purchase them directly from Blay because he couldn't meet Magnetic Video's $8,000 minimum wholesale order.

Video rental was a new market, and Atkinson was not sure if it was even legal. Magnetic Video's tapes had been sold "for home use only," and with Fox and other studios poised to enter the video market themselves, it seemed to Atkinson that he could be in a legal grey area and could become a target of the studios. He called the FBI and the MPAA to ask, but got no concrete answers.

Soon, legal or not, the video rental industry blossomed. In the days before a Blockbuster store on every corner, the video rental business was quite literally a cottage industry, or perhaps more precisely, given it was the late 1970s, a strip mall storefront industry. There were few barriers to entry. Entrepreneurs who had a few thousand dollars could buy the stock of tapes they needed and set up business. Many video stores set up membership programs, in which customers had to purchase annual or lifetime memberships, as a way of reducing the risk of video theft as well as capitalizing a cash-strapped startup. In the days when video renting was new, video stores could get away with this. Renting videos became extraordinarily popular, and VCR prices plummeted by the late 1970s. Indeed, by 1980 the production of prerecorded tapes exceeded three million units, from a base of zero only five years earlier.[14] The rental market became obvious even to the studios. Many studios devised plans to muscle in on the growing market. Several tried to devise rental schemes whereby they would lease videos to rental stores who in turn would rent them out. The studios had hoped to gain recurring revenue for themselves and tempt cash-strapped mom-and-pop video rental businesses by reducing the cash-flow burden they faced.

The operators making up the rental industry were a disparate lot, but one thing they did agree on is that they did not like the studio's leasing schemes. They found the terms intrusive as well as insufficiently lucrative. Indeed, the monitoring costs, given the state of computerized inventory tracking technology at the time, might have sunk the deal had the video operators been more receptive. In any event, after much acrimony, the studios abandoned their plans.

To gain more revenue from the video rental market, studios developed a two-tiered pricing system, not unlike the A and B theater system developed in the early days of the industry, in which new releases to video would be priced high and aimed at the rental market. Later the same title would be priced lower for the home library market. Over time, the video rental market had consolidated, with only half of the twenty thousand video rental outlets owned by independent retailers or small chains and the rest controlled by large chains such as Blockbuster and Hollywood Video.[15] With power shifted, in 1998 Blockbuster and other large chains initiated revenue-sharing contracts with studios. These arrangements consisted of an up-front fee per tape (ranging from nothing to $8) and a revenue split paid on the basis of rental revenue. Studios typically earned between 40 percent and 60 percent of rental revenues.[16] The revenue sharing was profitable for both video rental chains and the studios. In 1999, studios collected more than $16 billion from videocassette sales and rentals. That figure represented 55 percent of domestic studio revenues, making it their largest single cash source. By comparison, the studios made only 22 percent of their annual revenue from the box office and 23 percent from all other channels, such as pay-per-view, cable, and broadcast television.[17] (Interestingly, studios had also been wary of selling their films to cable television broadcasters when they first emerged, fearing that cable TV would keep people away from the movie theaters.)

Fast forward to today, and home video (video tapes and DVDs) sales have become essential to the economics of the film industry. Studios found that the home market presented opportunities to make money from films that did not do well at the box office. (My wife will see a trailer for a film that only mildly interests her and will whisper to me, "that's a renter," meaning that she won't fork out the price of admission but would be willing to rent the DVD.) And the channel was growing; spending on home entertainment rose 18.5 percent to $22.5 billion in 2003. Consumers in the United States spent $9.2 billion on movies at the box office, but spent more than twice that amount to purchase and rent videos and DVDs at home.[18] This channel may have compressed the "theatrical window" during which movies are exhibited in theaters, and the ease with which pirated copies of movies can be transmitted has meant that studios no longer have the luxury of releasing popular movies in regular and staggered dates, hitting the United States first, Western Europe a few months later, and so on. But the rewards presented by the new technologies seem well worth the challenges to the business model.

HAPPIER BEDFELLOWS: CONTENT-TECHNOLOGY COOPERATION

Although the cable television industry does not enjoy a sterling reputation in the United States (particularly for service), it does offer an excellent example of how cooperation between distribution technologies and content owners can be achieved for the benefit of both parties as well as consumers.

Cable television began in the late 1940s as a method of bringing broadcast television to areas with poor television reception, due to terrain—for example—mountains, or distance from broadcast stations. One early cable entrepreneur, John Walson, was the owner of a television and appliance shop in Mahanoy City, Pennsylvania, a town situated in the Allegheny Mountains. The beautiful mountain scenery interfered with the reception of television broadcast signals, which was a drag on the sales of television sets. In 1948, to spur sales, this entrepreneur built an antenna on a nearby peak to capture broadcast television signals. He offered a wire connection to this antenna to purchasers of his television sets, for a small connection charge and a monthly subscription. Thus a $200 billion business in the United States was born.

Until the late 1960s, most cable operators were retransmitting broadcast signals, in effect extending the range of a television station. However, as the industry grew, it attracted the attention of regulators, such as the FCC, which sought to control it, and television broadcasters, who worried about the effects of cable operators on their growing network of affiliates. Broadcast television companies twice sued community antenna television (CATV) stations over CATV retransmission of broadcast television signals. In two important cases in 1968 and 1974, courts found that CATV stations could retransmit broadcasts without violating any copyrights.[19] These findings greatly helped the development of cable television in the United States.

In the 1970s, cable television began to offer more than retransmitted broadcast television signals. In 1975, premium cable networks began to emerge. Cable operators charged subscribers an additional fee, around $8–$10 per month on top of the monthly subscription fee, for access to premium cable networks. Cable companies paid the premium network about $3–$5 for each subscriber and an additional fee for every increment charged to subscribers over a set amount.[20] Cable networks such as HBO, owned by Time, Inc., began offering exclusive programming, including blockbuster sporting events not regularly covered by television such as the Muhammad Ali-Joe Frazier bout known as the "Thrilla in Manila." The public ate this up, and by 1975, almost 13 percent of households in the United States subscribed to cable.

Movies quickly followed on the heels of sports. HBO and Showtime began showing more films, and new premium networks were launched that showed only movies. This provided a valuable new market for studios at the same time that VCRs were creating an additional new market for their content. Cable networks aired movies in the window after they had finished their theatrical release and before their release on tape.

Several studios tried in 1979 to get into the action directly, by joining together to form a cable movie channel called Premier, but the Justice Department, considering it a violation of antitrust laws, got an injunction against the fledgling network. These were familiar charges against Hollywood and one probable reason studios did not get into the industry earlier.

Instead studios ended up working well with the cable companies to develop encryption technologies and standards and devise revenue-sharing schemes that spread the wealth. Similar cooperation between content providers and online distributors and their complements, such as PC makers, has been much slower to develop.

Yet this cooperative paradigm is precisely what is needed to deal with the challenges and opportunities created by digitization. For example, the industry group CableLabs, a nonprofit research and development consortium serving the cable industry, researches and develops new cable telecommunications technologies and helps cable operators (who support the operation with dues of 1 cent per subscriber) integrate technical advancements into their businesses. CableLabs works with everybody in the industry, players such as Microsoft, Real Networks, and Tivo as well as companies specializing in conditional access and digital rights management, to develop workable solutions to the problems of piracy. It is telling of the myopia of Hollywood that studios work mostly with the cable operators (their customers) rather than develop technology and standards earlier in the stream. Recording companies have not been present at all in this collaborative effort, even though the fat cables that can bring movies and phone service to consumers, and are already in-stalled in about 60 percent of the homes in the United States, could easily support some kind of legal music distribution channel.

It is important to note that the interests of the cable industry and the en-tertainment industry are closely aligned here. Things are more complex for the PC industry. Although we have seen that the PC industry and entertain-ment industry are complements to each other, there are a couple of significant points of friction between the two. The PC industry often accuses the enter-tainment industry of trying to use copyright issues—specifically the so-called antipiracy technologies—to limit the power and flexibility of PCs, which are rapidly moving from being manipulators of spreadsheets and documents to becoming powerful, multifunctional entertainment devices. Some PC indus-try critics say Hollywood wants the government to force PC manufacturers to make "brain dead" PCs that nobody will want to buy in order to protect the ever-expanding copyrights enjoyed by Hollywood. Meanwhile the entertain-ment industry accuses PC makers of aiding and abetting piracy by making powerful machines without consideration of copyright protections for the content they run. The unease felt by the PC industry over the copyright issue is heightened by the fact that this industry itself is very reliant on copyright protections to secure the massive investments it must make in R&D.

The cable television industry in the United States (that is, the companies that actually own the cable and other infrastructure as opposed to content providers who use cable as a conduit) was never known for cutting-edge tech-nology, nor was it famous for investing more than what was absolutely neces-sary to provide service at (and unfortunately sometimes below) minimally acceptable standards, but its members fund and maintain research consortia that produce useful technological results and standards. Imagine what would be possible if the likes of Disney, Intel, and Dell, along with the MPAA and the RIAA managed to put away their daggers for a moment and cooperated out of enlightened self-interest. They, consumers, and the United States economy would surely all be winners.

THE MUSIC INDUSTRY POST-NAPSTER

After the demise of Napster in 2001, other free filesharing programs quickly emerged to take its place. Napster, a hybrid P-to-P service with centralized servers, had been easy to shut down. The next generation of filesharing networks, such as Gnutella (an open-source network shared by users of the software programs written for it: Morpheus, BearShare, and LimeWire) and FastTrack (a proprietary network hosting the users of Grokster, KaZaa, and iMesh), were true P-to-P programs, operating without central servers. With true P-to-P software, users could search for music files residing directly on other users' computers without being directed by a centralized server. This network structure made responsibility for illegal music files (and litigation targets) more diffuse. Most of the P-to-P networks sustained themselves for a time through advertising revenue, but litigators increasingly tied these companies up in court. Even though the labels became savvier about otherwise preventing their content from being shared illegally, providing content for legitimate subscription-based download services as an alternative, and companies and universities began limiting filesharing activity, P-to-P networks continued to thrive. The recording industry won some gains, for example arch-enemy KaZaa went legitimate in July 2006, agreeing to pay $100 million in damages to the industry. Legal downloads accounted for 6 percent of 2005 annual revenue for the industry. Also, the rate of illegal downloading of music seemed to flatten by 2005. Still, an estimated 20 billion tracks had been downloaded since Napster emerged.[21]

Subscription Services[22]

Simultaneously, the record labels launched their initial efforts to provide legitimate alternatives to the P-to-P networks. In December 2001, Pressplay (a joint venture between Sony and UMG) and MusicNet (a joint venture between AOL Time Warner, Bertelsmann AG, and EMI) were launched. Both offered a monthly subscription service in exchange for different tiers of access to online songs. Subscription rates ranged from $9.95 to $14.95 per month. These first incarnations of subscription services received mixed reviews from users who could not access as many songs as were available on P-to-P networks. However, over the past couple of years the labels increased the number of songs available on these services. They have also embarked upon various other digital distribution services via third- party agreements (such as UMG's distribution agreement with TowerRecords.com, whose parent company Tower Records announced it was going out of business in 2006, and other click-and-mortar retail distributors to sell digital tracks online).

By early 2003, the industry had begun launching version 2.0 of its online subscription services. Tom Sturges, executive vice president of creative affairs at Universal Music Publishing Group, and a thoughtful observer of and participant in the recording industry, reflected on the industry's initial inability to capitalize on filesharing. "This was the first time that the music business did not take advantage of a new technology. When we moved from LPs to cassettes, sales grew. From cassettes to CDs, sales grew. Some major players believe we lost the digital distribution opportunity altogether by not embracing Napster when we had a chance. Napster had collected 45 million fans into a community. These were centralized users—not distributed over P-to-P networks in multiple places. They loved music and, who knows, might have paid for the service Napster had to offer." While some music industry executives continued to compare filesharing to theft, seeing it as a threat, Sturges saw parallels with the business's other marketing efforts. "What is MTV? What is radio? They are fantastic marketing and promotion vehicles via which the music industry introduces its new talent to the world. That's all Napster was. But why was it perceived so differently and why were we unable to see the potential benefits?"[23]

Amanda Marks, senior vice president, Universal Music Group/e-Labs, a colleague of Tom Sturges, and a thoughtful industry observer herself, said it wasn't that easy. Once the labels began to recognize the potential for digital distribution, they had a gargantuan task ahead of them, especially those such as UMG with aggressive digital distribution plans. "We are the biggest music company with the most to lose, so it is incumbent upon us to transform all our business processes for digital distribution."[24]

Specifically, the company undertook massive efforts to digitize and metatag (code that describes the content of the work so that full attribution is available for recovering royalties) on a track-by-track level, thus adding new infrastructure while converting legacy systems and feeding these into the company's new digital distribution support system. These steps were necessary to make track-by-track sales a reality. For example, said Marks, "We had to tag each track with unique identifiers so each could flow through the royalty system, paying artists accordingly. For instance, on a Billie Holliday Greatest Hits album there could be three different versions of the same song, and a different trail of royalty participants for each, with different payment setups for the different producers and musicians on each different track."[25]

Moreover, the scale was enormous, because the company had committed itself to making its entire active catalog (110,000 tracks, excluding classical, which were not in the legacy systems) available to customers via à la carte downloads. By March 2003 UMG had approximately 70,000 tracks online. Marks recounted the strides e-Labs had made: "We're proud of having already made over 70,000 tracks available to the marketplace through 30 or so affiliate sites and services—the largest volume seen so far—and aiming for the full active catalog by end of 2003. Also, we were the first to come out with tens of thousands of tracks at $0.99, a price we thought would be in the consumers' sweet spot."[26]

UMG and the other labels continued their steady progress toward robust digital distribution catalogs, but their efforts were slowed by structural challenges in certain segments. One problem was establishing efficient handling of micropayments (small charges) for online music consumption. For example, teenagers, who are traditionally the most avid music buyers, do not typically possess credit cards, the primary method of payments for subscription services. The labels had invested heavily to develop teen recording stars, but the teen segment could not always follow through to purchase for this reason. Not surprisingly, the market research firm Ipsos Insight reported that, "Total file-sharing remains constant, with teens driving adoption" of illicit downloaders of titles by those same teen stars.[27]

Several of the initial proprietary attempts at subscription services received criticism from users. Both MusicNet and Pressplay were criticized for their overly complex software, confusing price schemes, limited inventory (rolling out only a small number of tracks at launch date), limited song portability (the inability to copy songs to portable devices), and difficulties moving memberships and music from one computer to another. Some services provided only tethered downloads, limiting use of a track to the duration of the user's subscription. This characteristic irked those consumers who for so long had been accustomed to "owning" the music once purchased through traditional retail distributors. Critics said it seemed that these services were overseen by executives more concerned with "locking down" content than distributing it.

By the middle of 2003, the labels, and a new entrant onto the scene, Apple Computer's iTunes music download service, had begun to make real headway in providing reasonably priced and comprehensive music download services. Still, an estimated 1.2 million unique tracks were available through fileswapping services, and market research firm Ipsos estimated that twenty million Americans had engaged in filesharing during December 2002 alone.[28]

During 2002, the record labels and technology companies began to resolve some of their disputes. Both Microsoft and RealNetworks, the developers of the two competing leading media player software applications, inched closer to Hollywood by promising to include additional content safeguards in their technologies. Previously, the general attitude at some technology companies had been to access content with little regard for copyright protection. Amanda Marks anticipated the day when consumers could have secure, easy access to their music files: "Ultimately, we would love to have CDs with pre-ripped second-session files so that, with the click of a mouse, you could easily transfer music tracks to a computer or a portable device. Right now, though many are working on finding a solution, none of the various technology companies have yet provided something that is really viable. No one thinks you can stop CD piracy 100 percent, but stopping 70 to 80 percent of casual piracy would be nice."[29]

Other music executives are more sanguine about piracy. Brad Serling, the founder and CEO of Nugs.net, an innovative company that sells full-length recordings of rock concerts online, either from downloads or streaming from its Website, discussed piracy in an interview in the *New York Times:* "People who are intent on ripping you off are going to rip you off no matter what you do." Serling dismissed DRM measures as the "number 1 issue that most of the music industry has wrong," because it restricts the freedom of legitimate consumers to enjoy their purchases in the ways they wish (for example, listening on a stereo, or on a PC, or on a digital music player, and so on), out of fear that some illegitimate users will be able to pirate their wares.[30]

In 2004, with the recording industry entering its fourth year of declining sales, and with the overwhelming majority of music downloads illegal, despite the presence of fast-growing legal sites, it was tempting for the recording industry to blame piracy spread via illegal downloading for their woes. However, new research has suggested that illegal filesharing has no discernable effect on music sales, at most being responsible for only a tiny fraction of the decline in music sales. These findings, if they hold up to further scrutiny, would mean that the technological speed bumps being considered, such as stringent DRM techniques, as well as the terrible public relations from RIAA lawsuits against consumers are all for naught. The fall-off in record sales could be explained by phenomenon such as the reduction in the number of album releases, growing competition from other forms of electronic entertainment (such as video games), and even the reduction in variety of music played over the airwaves stemming from the consolidation of radio stations into massive networks such as Clear Channel.[31] Other researchers thought piracy did have a profound impact on record sales, with some analysts estimating that the worldwide recording industry lost an estimated $2.4 billion in sales due to illegal downloads.[32] Still other researchers pointed to similar declines in record sales in the late 1970s and early 1980s and speculated that the comparatively high level of record sales in the 1990s may have been, in large part, a function of consumers replacing music on older formats (such as vinyl albums and tapes) with CDs.[33]

Online music provider RealNetworks offers an interesting example of the way companies can innovate around large obstacles. The company provided software that allowed computer users to easily play music and other content on PCs. The business benefited from the explosion in filesharing ignited by Napster and its cousins. However, the company also found itself in the sights of Microsoft, and faced getting embraced and extended out of existence as Microsoft included its own media player, a substitute for the RealNetworks product, in the popular Windows operating system, which runs on more than 95 percent of all PCs. Instead of facing the same fate as browser pioneer and erstwhile Internet success story Netscape, that is, getting bought and languishing somewhere in a conglomerate, RealNetworks changed its business model. Instead of relying on software sales, the company now relies on subscription revenue from users who pay for the content it provides, such as NBA games and NASCAR races. It is very similar to a cable business model. In addition, with some of the music roadblocks finally out of the way, RealNetworks also sells music, by the download and through subscriptions. Its Rhapsody music download service competes with Apple's iTunes and the now-legal Napster as the most popular legitimate music sites.

Rhapsody and iTunes developed exciting business models for the consumption of digital music. Some, such as iTunes, favored a pay-per-song business model in which consumers kept the music on their devices (PCs or iPods, and so on). Others, such as Rhapsody, used mostly subscription models in which the music was not stored on any device but instead streamed to the consumer. In any event, the opportunity to have legal online channels vastly improved the experience of consuming music for consumers.

Another issue that the music industry was getting wrong—again—was royalty fees for songs played over the Internet. Until 2004, the recording industry had lobbied the U.S. Copyright Office to set royalty fees for Webcasters, radio stations that broadcast over the Internet, higher than those paid by traditional radio stations. Since the late 1990s, Webcasters had been struggling to get off the ground. The recording industry's fee demand seemed designed to thwart the development of a new distribution channel for music (stop me if you heard this before). The Copyright Office agreed upon a compromise that was less than the recording studios had asked for, but still more than traditional radio stations have to pay for the same material.[34] Even so, the industry seemed like it was finally getting traction and developing more robust revenue models as more listeners tuned in to radio broadcasts over the Internet. Webcasters are responsible for an important, and growing, amount of royalty revenue for artists and labels.

CONCLUSION

The surest ticket to the Prosperity stage has always been to give consumers new and profitable ways to enjoy content. This is often what new technologies do. However, as we have seen in the past it has not always been immediately clear to content owners how they would prosper from the new technologies. Technology companies either because they were too nascent to have clout or disinterested did not seek compromises or help develop business models that would compel content owners to come along on the wave of technological change. Content owners usually did not understand the impact of new technologies and lacked sufficient imagination until somebody showed them the way to Prosperity. Interestingly, the barriers to mutual understanding between technology and content can exist even when the two groups are housed within the same company. I recall one very senior executive from a conglomerate of content distributors and technology assets telling me how pleased he was that broadband adoption was so slow in the United States because he feared piracy, never considering the drag that slow broadband adoption had on so many of the assets of the company.

When content and technology overcame their suspicions of each other and realized that they could cooperate to create new and valuable distribution channels for content, then everybody benefited.

Today's technologies pose even greater opportunities and challenges. These technological forces have the power to atomize content, break it up into smaller pieces that are still compelling to consumers, and deliver it to an ever-growing variety of devices. This atomization can be a less cheerful phenomenon in comparison with the so-called "long tail" effect.[35] Some of the same forces that enable low-friction transactions—allowing profitable sales of low-demand items at the far end (long tail) of the demand distribution curve—also break up or atomize established products and services. This atomization can mean a company only makes a dime where it used to make a dollar, because it sells only a small piece of its former product, for example, a single song instead of a CD. But it can also mean that atomized content can be sold in new ways that will allow content owners to make many, many more dimes. Success will hinge on the company's ability to find new products, services, and channels that are created by atomization. Today, even more courage, vision, and self-interest will be needed to see these forces as complements and not threats.

6 CONCLUSION

EIGHTY YEARS AGO, the Coca Cola Company decided its mission was to place a bottle of coke "within an arm's reach of desire." Coke did not take Henry Ford's famous early approach to customer satisfaction (you can have a Model T in any color you want, as long as it is black) and offer only twelve-ounce bottles. Instead it made Coke available everywhere and in a wide variety of forms: cans, bottles, fountains, you name it.

Imagine if Coke had struggled mightily against new distribution methods such as steel and later aluminum cans, or plastic two-liter bottles. As we have seen, that is essentially what content owners did time and again: from sheet music to records to TV to VCR, each innovation was fought vigorously by the companies that owned the content to fill those vessels and stood to gain the most from their deployment.

Technology enables content companies to offer their products to consumers in new ways. But usually the content companies resist because the changes upset their established ways of doing business. Instead of seeing a complement, content companies usually saw a competitor and receded into the Fear state, trying to stomp on an innovation that had already passed through Ascension.

What the recording industry has been doing over the past almost twenty years—until iTunes and its cousins entered the picture—is the equivalent of offering only two-liter bottles, forcing consumers to pay $15–$17 for a CD of around ten tracks. They could get away with this because consumers had few alternatives, until technology changed the environment and digitized music could be traded and downloaded over the Internet.

This shortsightedness is natural; most people are afraid of change, and changing one's business model, especially when times are bad, can be particularly nerve-wracking. So we can look back, mildly amused, at the misadventures of ASCAP, movie and television studios, and more recently music companies. Up until now these parties eventually learned to benefit from the changes in technology and ultimately were drawn into the Prosperity stage by better serving consumers in new ways. We could buy records and play them at home on our phonographs, we could watch old movies on TV, we could use VCRs to watch favorite movies or record programs and games we would have otherwise missed, and we could listen to music on CDs with a high level of fidelity impossible to achieve from vinyl albums or tapes. In each case, technology made things more convenient for the consumer and more value was created from activities previously unimagined (such as watching favorite movies at home on your own schedule), all creating more wealth for the content owners who had previously resisted the technologies that ended up making them so much money.

In the past, content companies have been able eventually to work with the complement to find prosperity. Today's technology is not so patient. The technological forces that drive most of the changes described in this book, such as digitization, Moore's Law, networking, and broadband, offer tremendous opportunities for content owners to create new distribution channels and even new types of content. These forces create new ways for consumers to enjoy this content. But these same forces also erase many of the advantages enjoyed by incumbents and overcome industry boundaries that have been established over decades, within which predictable business models and value chains have been established.

Taken together, these forces have the power not only to alter established value chains in entertainment but to completely recreate them. We have seen in this book that companies and industries that eventually intuited their way through the Fear stage and into Prosperity were able to benefit from new technologies. The technologies today are as impatient as they are powerful, and companies and industries that fail to understand them and allow themselves to stay in the Fear stage too long will find they become at best marginalized and at worst out of business.

To be successful in a technological environment shaped by the forces described in this book, content industries and technology industries will have to become a lot cozier with each other. They will have to display enlightened self-interest in cooperating with each other in a couple of important areas. In particular, they will need to jointly (and meaningfully) fund research efforts, probably along the lines of an industrial consortium, to devise and promulgate agreeable technological standards and solutions to a few key problems. These include standards for digital rights management, which protect copyrighted material from much copying while protecting the rights of the vast majority of consumers who are not pirates or shoplifters (to use the favorite metaphor of the RIAA). These standards and tools will give copyright owners greater security in exploiting their property and technology companies increased demand for new products and services as consumers enjoy the benefits of imagined and yet unimagined ways of consuming human creativity. The efforts in this area to date largely have been anemic at best and counterproductive at worst.

The fact that in 2006 two competing standards entered the market for high-definition DVD with various movie studios and technology companies lining up behind one or the other shows that many key players have not understood this lesson of enlightened (and legal) cooperation on technology standards. Now it looks like consumers will be subjected to the same wasteful standards battle they faced with the Betamax-VHS contest that played out in the 1980s.

In one way or another, government will play a big role, for good or for ill, in the way regulatory forces and consumer broadband uptake evolve over the coming years. Direct congressional involvement in setting standards or capabilities for devices, such as mandating code in semiconductors that prevents copying, is likely to generate the least amount of good for consumers and technologies and even in the short term is likely to be unhelpful for content owners. As we have seen, the recording industry and the movie industry should be thankful that time and again they have been saved from themselves and their own shortsightedness by past courts and Congresses that viewed the "copyright glass as half-full for consumers." Because they did, the new distribution channels that were created overflowed with profits for their recalcitrant content owners. Content owners are at it again, proposing legislation that could throttle growth, for both their own industries and their complements: the technology sector as a whole. But this time, because of the power of the forces that govern distribution, they may be partially correct in their concerns, and government will likely be part of any solution.

For example, there is a role for government to play in encouraging better and faster consumer broadband deployment, an area in which the United States is not the global leader but twelfth in the world in the percentage of its population that has broadband Internet access at home.[1] In the United States, the FCC oversees the implementation of the 750,000-word telecommunications statute. Federal courts become involved when there is disagreement over the FCC's interpretation of telecommunications law. And there are plenty of disagreements, sometimes over basic philosophy, such as what the role of government should be in telecommunications and media in general, and sometimes over what to even call a thing. For example, much rides on whether consumer broadband access is categorized as "telecommunications" or "information" services. If it is a telecommunications service, under the United States Telecommunications Act of 1996 it would be highly regulated. In 2003, the FCC determined that broadband was an information service, making it subject to looser regulation. Soon after, a court ruled that it was a hybrid service that included a telecommunications component. This would make broadband subject to a range of regulations.

Opponents of classifying broadband services as information services argue that regulations are necessary to ensure that broadband companies do not restrict access to the Internet. One danger they cite is that a cable broadband or DSL provider could force consumers to use Internet service providers that they own or with which they have commercial agreements. The Coalition of Broadband Users and Innovators, whose members include consumer groups, trade associations, and companies such as Microsoft and Amazon.com, argue that broadband providers could "implement restrictions designed to block or impair access to innovative content, services and devices on the broadband network."[2]

This is not theoretical. In China, the popular search engine Google is classified as a media company and access is restricted. Until recently, Webpages served by Google to users in China had to pass through filters set up by the Chinese government that eliminate information the State does not want people to see. In 2006, Google announced that it would set up a local site in China, to better serve the China market. The site would feature only "sanitized" search results that met the approval of the Chinese government. So next time you are in Beijing, try searching for Falun Gong, the social group that so upsets the ruling party, and see what, if anything you get. While this kind of censorship is odious to many of us, the Chinese government is right to think that Google is a media company. It is. And so are Yahoo, MSN, YouTube, MySpace, and any number of companies that have sprung up in the ground fertilized by forces such as Moore's Law, networking, and digitization. These forces have combined to create something that is new and powerful. Regardless of your political stripe, Democrat, Republican, or especially Chinese Communist Party, the power created by the combination of these forces is tremendous.

WHERE THE MONEY *WILL* BE: THE POWER OF COMPLEMENTS AND THE RISKS OF COLLISION

The biggest potential benefit of the changes described in this book is the ability of content and technology to be powerful complements for each other.

Just as Microsoft and Intel complemented each other in the technology standard known as "Wintel" and we ended up with going on two billion PCs on desktops and laps and ignited a revolution that is putting powerful PC-like devices into the palm of your hand (think of cell phones, PDAs such as the BlackBerry, and iPods), the power of complements means there are vast opportunities for technology and content to be more valuable together.

Some TV networks are determined not to repeat the mistakes of the recording industry and ignore technological complements, even though the business model for exploiting them is not yet clear. For example, ABC (owned by Disney) and NBC (owned by General Electric) began offering new episodes of television shows for sale on iTunes for $1.99, and CBS (owned by Viacom) offers old shows as well as content created specifically for the Web for free on its (advertising supported) Innertube Website and rents some shows commercial-free for various prices starting under $1.

These are the kinds of experiments that TV networks need to do. There is not one clear winning business model—for example, iTunes lets you own the content, CBS rents the content—and probably consumers will want a choice. That is a decision they should be allowed to make. It should not be imposed upon them by third parties such as Congress through some misguided DRM scheme or by oligopolistic fiat (such as the consolidating entertainment industry could become).

The networks' affiliates are the ones with the most at risk and who are the least able to exploit the new technology. For example, affiliates are likely to lose out on ad revenue if viewers choose to watch the good bits of *Saturday*

Night Live on YouTube instead of waiting until 11:30 P.M. to watch the broadcast on their local NBC affiliate. Like networks, affiliates make money by carrying local advertising. If fewer people watch an affiliate's broadcast, it makes less money in advertising. As you might imagine, affiliates are a powerful force in the television networks' value chain. It seems pretty clear that affiliates will lose power over time to alternative distribution channels such as the Internet. But until that happens, affiliates are important enough to make the networks feel their pain. Some networks are looking for creative ways to try to share online ad revenue with affiliates, but the writing is on the wall: technology undermines the power of network affiliates and changes the balance of power between networks and affiliates that has developed over the past fifty years.

In fact, distributors of all kinds who have relied on physical assets such as chains of stores or regulatory assets such as broadcast spectrum in a given city and region are very close to the sharp end of the technological changes discussed in this book. Taken together, among other things, these changes reduce the cost of distribution. Still, stores such as Wal-Mart are vital channels for movie DVD and music CD sales, and network affiliates are responsible for distributing the content aired by broadcast television networks. Therefore, movie studios, record companies, and television networks have to tread lightly as they adjust their value chains to exploit technological forces. Nevertheless, changes will have to be made.

CONVERGENCE OR COLLISION?

For the industries discussed in this book, the confluence of forces such as Moore's Law, client-server computing, and the Internet together have a very large impact upon the way that information industries do business. Where these forces touch existing businesses, there is less convergence and more "collision" (to quote Intel former CEO and chairman Andy Grove, a more astute observer than most). And where such big forces collide, somebody is going to get hurt. Until now, it was the recording companies that have suffered massive declines in sales, some but not all of which is probably attributable to illegal filesharing. The movie industry has been looking at the recording industry's experience with dread, fearing that they will be the next to suffer a similar fate. But consumers too have been hurt by the collision. Content owners have, until very recently, been reluctant to even explore online distribution of their products. This has left a vacuum only partially filled by illegal filesharing, and stalled the uptake of consumer broadband access, which in turn has stalled the sales of PCs. If email is the best thing out there on the Internet, why do I need a fast connection and anything better than a Pentium 4?

The result of some of this collision is a drag on price. Universal Music cut the suggested retail price of its CDs to $10. While Microsoft is in nowhere near the critical condition of the recording industry, it too has been affected by these forces. There are significant parallels between the recording industry and the experience of Microsoft and Linux Operating System and the open source community, the loosely knit group of software developers around the world that donated their time and intellectual sweat to create Linux. Both Linux and most peer-to-peer filesharing sites are self-organizing communities. Whereas individual developers contribute code to Linux, individuals contribute content to P-to-P sites (granted that much of that content is illegal because it violates copyright law). The effects on incumbents have been similar. Linux has forced Microsoft to contain pricing for server operating systems, and filesharing has forced some record companies to drop CD pricing and use legal download services, such as Apple's iTunes, which unbundled the CD and set the price of a song at 99 cents. Even middle-America retail giant Wal-Mart got in on the act, setting up an online music store that offered songs for 88 cents.

If more evidence is needed about the difficulties of the current recording industry business model, consider this: some legal download sites charge more to download an album than it cost to buy the same (physical) CD from Amazon. Consumers want this channel: 25 million digital tracks were sold in the first three months of 2004, compared with 19.2 million sold in all of 2003.[3] By late 2003, roughly one billion songs were downloaded each week; mostly illegally. The numbers continued to grow.

It is becoming increasingly clear that the recording industry, as it is structured today, could disappear. It could turn out to be unsustainable as a discrete industry, or even as part of a larger media conglomerate. Some speculate that the recording industry could become a loss-leader for the consumer electronics industry. They have a point. Margins in online music distribution, such as Apple's iTunes, are razor thin for the recording industry and for Apple. According to reports, Apple pays 77 cents for songs it sells for 99 cents.[4] Still, both the recording industry and Apple greatly benefit from iTunes. For the recording industry, iTunes proved that users would pay for downloaded music and established the first compelling legal alternative to Napster and its ilk. For Apple, iTunes drives sales of its pricey and highly profitable iPods.

HONEY, I SHRUNK THE VALUE PROPOSITION

The forces described in this book enable content to be enjoyed in more and more varied ways. What is different, new, and exciting about these forces is that they combine to fundamentally change the way content can be consumed. Specifically, the base purchase unit of digital content, particularly entertainment, can be reduced. Because the cost of delivering digitized information is so low (for example, via the Internet instead of through a brick-and-mortar distribution network), and mechanisms for consuming it are becoming ever more compelling (for example, ever thinner and lighter laptop computers with better pictures and sound, ever-cheaper digital televisions, mobile phones with improving picture screens, video iPods, and so on), wholly new avenues of consumption are becoming available.

This allows value to be extracted from content in ways that were not possible in the past. For example, snippets of songs or favorite scenes from movies can be used for mobile phone ringtones (can you just imagine a mobile phone that instead of the annoyingly common ringtones has Robert De Niro's voice asking "You talkin' to me?" à la *Taxi Driver*?). There is a universe of possibilities for things as yet unimagined. This offers challenges and opportunities to content owners. When your livelihood has been based on the sale of a collection of songs on an album (or CD) or on the exhibition of a movie in a theater it can be difficult to embrace a new business model. Like the generals of World War I who disastrously used well-understood but outmoded tactics in the face of new mechanized weapons, which led to trench-war stalemate, content owners have instead gone to Congress to extend copyright over and over again, and have tried to outlaw the technologies that they feel are threatening. As we saw in the Fear chapter, this has also led to a kind of stalemate; one that is slowly being resolved, but not in the best interests of consumers.

There is plenty of blame to be shared by content owners, Congress, the technology industry, and consumers. Yes, consumers too have contributed to the problem. Copying beyond legitimate provisions of fair use is wrong. Period. Downloading copyrighted songs through illegal filesharing services is very much like shoplifting. The fact that the copyright owners in the past had been too stupid to provide a credible alternative does not make it legal or ethical to download tracks or movies. Such consumers do deserve censure, but should not be hit with the sledgehammer that the RIAA and others have tried to wield against this problem. It is not good business sense to sue your potential customers; similarly, it is not good business sense to make your customers detest your industry. Suing teenagers for downloading songs and sponsoring lame trailers before movies with the heartfelt reminder that when you buy a pirated film you are really hurting the everyday craftspeople (forget about overpaid stars and rapacious producers) are not solutions. They are part of the same old trench warfare that is inhibiting the development of new content and new ways of enjoying content that we consumers are waiting for.

The problems are not unsolvable. However, they require enlightened self-interest on the part of industries that are powerful, a Congress that has lost its way on copyright, and consumers who want what they want now.

The common theme running throughout this book has been control. Each new technology discussed here has wrested control, for a time, from the owners of content. The technologies created new markets for content, and eventually content owners learned to understand and exploit these markets. This is when VCRs go from being the "Boston Strangler" to a studio's best friend. However, today, navigating this bumpy road has been made even more challenging.

How should technology companies or entertainment companies or the new type of "pushme-pullyou" companies (think of Google) that increasingly comprise both industries think about the future? To the extent that companies and industries can change some forces, such as copyright protection, but can't change other forces, such as Moore's Law, (it is easier to change regulations than physics), how should players in various industries prepare themselves, and how should they try to shape their futures?

In recent months, television broadcasters have been making some highly publicized, self-enlightened steps toward offering their content through new Internet-based delivery channels, for example via iTunes or over their own Websites. This is refreshing (and again, self-enlightened) because it gives freedom to consumers to pay for just what they consume, in the case of iTunes, or finds a good use for ad-supported Websites offered by TV broadcasters. It was only a few years ago that one respected broadcast television executive likened skipping commercials on shows that consumers recorded to stealing.[5] This was simply wrong. I agree with the observer who said that viewers have as much obligation to watch commercials as motorists have to look at billboards on the roadside.[6] Consumers will likely have a choice of roads to entertainment in the future, many of them Internet-based. The various toll booth operators will have to find new ways of collecting revenue.

The future of entertainment is being shaped today. It is being formed by Congress and consumers, movie studios, broadcast TV and cable networks, recording companies, technology companies such as Apple and Intel, and Internet companies such as Google (and its YouTube) but also BitTorrent (who saw those two coming a few years ago?). What kind of future should such disparate companies drive toward?

LET'S GET HORIZONTAL

As completely new technologies develop, their industries tend to be vertical, that is to say their constituent parts are made by the same companies. As described in Andy Grove's classic book *Only the Paranoid Survive,* the computer industry offers a good example of this.[7] During its first decades, computer companies generally supplied their own processors, operating systems, application software, and even sales and distribution arms. As the industry matured, industry-level standards developed for each of these layers that enabled third-party companies to offer products at each of these layers that could work together.

Different companies emerged that provided these components better or cheaper or both compared with vertically-integrated computer makers. As a result, the industry went horizontal; companies began to specialize in horizontal layers of the industry. For example, Microsoft specialized in operating systems and application software (Windows and Word), Intel specialized in microprocessors (Pentium and Centrino chips), and companies such as Dell and HP specialized in assembling and marketing computers. Because each company did what it did best, and because standards developed at each layer of the industry that allowed a variety of players to compete, horizontal structuring tended to make the entire industry more efficient, which lowered costs and prices. (Companies that developed proprietary control of important standards such as the "Wintel" standard for PC operating systems and microprocessor architecture benefited greatly from horizontal structuring.)

Today there is a debate about whether the horizontal model is best at the intersection of technology and content, a state that some call the post-PC era, in which the forces that made the PC great can be applied to devices considerably smaller than a desktop PC or even an ultra-mobile laptop computer.

The influential *Wall Street Journal* columnist Walter S. Mossberg has argued that in the post-PC environment, the end-to-end solution (a kind of vertical integration) so far has allowed for a better customer experience.[8] Mossberg cites the tight integration of hardware, software, and content found with Apple's iPod as evidence that vertical integration is the early winner in the first real killer app of the post-PC world. The elegance of the iPod and its software interface along with the ease of use of iTunes sharply contrasts with its competitors and their comparatively clunky devices and variety of online music stores that usually lack the simplicity of iTunes. Mossberg points out that although Apple used an end-to-end model with PCs and badly lost out to "Wintel," the end-to-end model might be just the ticket for the post-PC world.

Not surprisingly, Microsoft cofounder Bill Gates and Intel CEO Paul Otellini, themselves quite influential, fired back a rebuttal to Mossberg's column affirming their belief that the PC era is just getting started and that the horizontal model will continue to drive the most innovation in devices such as cell phones, digital players, and mobile PCs.[9]

For consumers, the semantic issue of whether today's intersection of technology and content represents a "post-PC era" or something like "PC 2.0" is not important, but the underlying issue discussed by Mossberg, Gates, and Otellini is a very big deal: that is whether or not the end-to-end, vertical industry structure offers consumers the best results at today's intersection of technology and content. Looking only at the iPod and its competitors, most consumers seem to be better served by Apple's model as evidenced by the iPod's overwhelming market share.

But the end-to-end model bets against history. The end-to-end vertical model wins only as long as the horizontal alternative is markedly inferior, as it is today. It is inferior because companies and indeed whole industries lack good understanding of the needs and technologies of their complements and have not made any meaningful efforts to alter or create new links in their value chains that would dramatically improve the resulting experience for end users.

For example, many consumer electronics companies have been hesitant to cast their support for existing "Wintel" standards because they do not want to be marginalized by that standard in the same way that PC makers were. After all, most of the industry profits for PCs went to Microsoft and Intel, which together controlled the vital "Wintel" standard. Unfortunately, these same consumer electronics companies have been unable to get behind an alternative standard for the coming era of the intersection of technology and content. That is why we are faced with wasteful standards battles such as the face-off between Blu-Ray and HD-DVD.

Apple's iPod and iTunes are undeniably elegant, but they look even better because their competitors are so bad. These competitors were brought together in a kind of shotgun wedding compelled by Apple's success. For Apple's competitors, the various elements of the digital music value chain do not sync up neatly because they were not designed to do so. The iPod proves that people will pay for good design and ease of use but it does not prove that the end-to-end model will dominate for long.

The risk to consumers of the end-to-end environment is that they get only the experience that the end-to-end provider cares to deliver. In Apple's hands lately that has been a pretty terrific experience at a reasonable price. But that could change. The risk to content providers, and ultimately a risk to consumers also, is that too much power shifts to the company that controls the end-to-end experience. For an example of this look at AOL back in the days when it was a "walled garden" and its content was selected more on the basis of which content providers would pay the most to be included in this walled garden than on what consumers really wanted to see. That might have been good enough for a large group of consumers when AOL was thought of as "the Internet on training wheels," but its end-to-end product was not a recipe for success as consumers matured and horizontal competitors such as Netscape's browser entered the picture with a compelling alternative.

If a company or industry can replicate enough of the benefits of the end-to-end solution (for example, the apparent seamlessness that translates into ease of use) and maintain the economic advantages of the horizontal structure, then you have a compelling alternative that seems destined to win. The first step toward replicating advantages of the end-to-end model is developing better linkages between the elements of an industry's value chain.

LINKING TO PROSPERITY: THE 2 PERCENT SOLUTION

Today, the forces affecting the content and technology industries are so powerful that entire value chains are up for grabs. Nobody can be sure how things will shake out for incumbents but what is clear is that the status quo will change, and soon.

What can executives do to manage this change? In short, how do you manage chaos, and how can a company or industry fight its way out of the Fear stage and into Prosperity?

It is vital that companies develop linkages between themselves and the technologies that they may see as competitors or that seem to make them uncomfortable. These linkages help ensure that companies are able to incorporate into their strategy-making the signals coming from the technologies and companies in the Innovation or Ascension stages of development. These linkages must be real, in that intelligence is transferred and decisions are made on the basis of this intelligence. Content companies do not need to become technology companies, nor do technology companies have to acquire content themselves. Indeed, simply bringing together such assets under one corporate roof is not sufficient. For example, Sony and Time Warner have both had much difficulty getting synergy from their combinations of technology and content.

For Sony, Time Warner, and indeed any content company, it is not enough for senior executives to watchfully wait (usually from a perch in the Fear stage); they must be receptive to and actively seek out signals coming from the Innovation and Ascension stages and be ready to evaluate and act on what they are told. If a company is going to benefit from technologies and new ways of doing business that are still in the Innovation and Fear stages—and ride them to prosperity—it must align its strategy-making processes to act on the opportunities it finds.

Content companies must devote a significant amount of resources to understanding technology and its impact on content. The exact amount depends upon many factors, but devoting around 2 percent of revenue to this specific kind of research and development (R&D) should be the starting point for discussions in content company boardrooms.

The purpose of this R&D is to find new ways to make content more valuable to consumers and new ways to distribute this content. The realities of the marketplace mean that powerful stakeholders, such as movie theaters, network television affiliates, and chains of retail stores, will need to be accommodated up to a point. This is a delicate balance. Perhaps the most difficult decision any established content company CEO will have to make over the next few years will be how far to accommodate entrenched channels of distribution and how aggressively to court or develop new channels. Companies in the Fear stage tend to push the balance in the direction of established channels.

To take full advantage of the converged future, technology companies will need to compete not on the basis of "lock-in" to some proprietary standard (like "Wintel") but rather on the ability of some particular piece of technology to provide a superior customer experience. To this end, they will have to be far more service-driven than they have been in the past. This will increasingly entail linking technology to a service that complements it. I would argue that the stunning success of iPods and iTunes has far more to do with the attractive design and ease of use of iPods and the comprehensiveness, and again ease of use, of the iTunes online music store along with its inexpensive and commonsense pricing plan for downloading songs than with any lock-in associated with Apple's proprietary standard.

Standards wars like the Betamax-VHS standoff or the current battle between competing high-definition DVD standards Blu-Ray and HD-DVD are costly and wasteful, and worst of all anger consumers and slow the adoption of a new technology. As we have seen, new technology can benefit everybody: consumers who want a new way to enjoy content, technology companies that make the new device, and content companies that make the material run on the new technology enjoyed by consumers.

Linkages will matter for technology companies too as they strive to make their technology work better with content sourced from various providers. By cooperating on standards, and spending money to create standards R&D labs that are supported by technology industries with cooperation from content industries, technologies can then compete on design and service, avoiding standards battles that are so wasteful. As with content companies, technology companies need to devote meaningful resources (financial and managerial) to developing common standards and improving the integration of a device and the service it is meant to perform.

RULES FOR SUCCESS: COMPANY-LEVEL VIEW

Seek, Listen to, and Act on Signals

At most companies, the top managers who make strategy are several steps removed in the organization chart from the employees who are most active in and attuned to developments or signals coming from companies and technologies in the Innovation or Ascension stages. Senior managers need to make sure they have mechanisms for soliciting intelligence from these people, evaluating it, acting on it, and rewarding it. They also need to ensure that at least some of their people have the appropriate technical and conceptual skills needed to work with the companies and technologies at the Innovation and Ascension stages. These people should be tasked with listening for signals that emerge in areas that are potential complements.

Beyond this, these same people need to have, or their managers must make sure they develop, the appropriate political skills to communicate within their own companies the intelligence they learn in their interactions with the Innovation and Ascension stages, especially to the top managers who create the firm's strategy. Too often in content industries such people will be seen as "geeks" while conversely, in the technology industries, people who really live and breathe content may be viewed skeptically by engineers or programmers.

Measure Revenue from New Sources

In practical terms the leaders of content companies and technology companies (and their boards of directors and discerning investors) should look for tangible proof that their companies are doing what it takes to succeed amid the forces discussed in this book. The most important metric is revenue from new channels and sources. While all revenue floats to the top line, not all revenue is equally meaningful in terms of measuring the success of a strategy. Content companies should have firm goals for earning some established percentage of revenue from entirely new applications of their content. Some technology companies should have similar goals for themselves in terms of creating or augmenting new delivery channels or methods of content consumption. These measures should become an important part of how executives and managers are evaluated and rewarded.

Learn to Profit from Atomization

Another way of thinking about this is to atomize yourself before somebody else does it for you (à la iTunes). Companies must create value propositions that take advantage of the way that new technologies allow content to be atomized. Given the ability of these technologies to break up physical elements in the entertainment industries' value chains, it is clear that an important source of new revenue for content companies and technology companies will be finding ways to make money from content that has been either broken up or purpose-built for consumption through a new technology.

Today, this means ringtones from songs and snippets of video played on computers and PDAs. But in the future, it will likely mean new and more robust opportunities for content and technology industries. These opportunities will come from new consumption and distribution technologies such as wireless broadband and display devices that combine formerly discrete functions performed by PCs, TVs, storage devices (for example, Tivo), and phones.

For the content industry powerful constituencies such as retail stores and television broadcast network affiliates will likely get hurt by this atomization. Because these are still powerful forces in the content industries' value chains, content companies will have to be very careful to initially try to share some benefits of atomization with these players. But an inevitable shift will take place because the economics of atomization are compelling and because it offers consumers more ways of consuming.

RULES FOR SUCCESS: INDUSTRY-LEVEL VIEW

Play Better Together

The first and easiest step will be for a meeting of the minds and checkbooks of content and technology leaders. This could take place in a consortium funded by entertainment and technology companies to research and develop digital rights technologies. Membership could be paid by a percentage of R&D spent (technology companies) or sales revenue made from sales (entertainment companies). This consortium would develop and promulgate DRM codes that will make copying protected material more difficult.

It is probably not economically feasible to develop commercial DRM solutions that are uncrackable. That is not the point. The goal should be to make it difficult for the casual copier to exceed the boundaries of fair use in illegally copying copyrighted material. The piecemeal solutions that are out there now, such as regional playback controls which make it impossible to play a DVD on computers or DVD players outside of a region such as Asia or North America, are anticonsumer and easily defeated. That is the problem with most of the anticopying technologies available today; they have been developed at the behest of one half of the duo of complementors, that is, the entertainment industry, and are overbroad, forcing legitimate consumers to use potentially illegal means to circumvent controls in order to consume the content in ways that are legal. Or the consumer must abandon many aspects of fair use entirely, for instance, forgoing the right to keep a backup of a legally purchased CD or DVD.

This consortium could also help industry players develop business models to capture the new and exciting ways of consuming content that are now (and soon will be) allowed by the forces described in this book. For example, a compelling legal alternative to Napster took three years to develop. This was a problem of vision (and the lack of will on the parts of the music industry), and not technology or public policy. Simply put, the recording industry could not come together to offer enough content in a legal way. Napster shined a bright light on the path, but the recording industry was more worried about shooting out the light than cashing in on the new opportunity. The industry had to wait until it was hemorrhaging before it put together a reasonable alternative.

Trim the Fig Leaf of Copyright Protection

There is a big role to be played by Congress too. It should severely reduce the length of copyright protection, to something closer to what prevailed in the first half of the twentieth century. The near limitless length of protection gives content owners a fig leaf of protection against relentless forces and stifles creativity. Ultimately, overlong terms of copyright protection limits the total value that can be gained from ideas through the recombination of existing content. The forces described allow content to be created and consumed in new ways, which will allow for greater wealth creation overall. The current copyright laws constrict this flexibility and have the effect of closing new avenues of consumption.

Collaborate with Your Complementors

In brief, technology companies and content owners need to play nicer with each other. The cable industry cooperative labs and development efforts are a good example of collaboration with complementors. These efforts help players understand the changes affecting the macroenvironment in which these players operate. Often the biggest changes are technological, which in turn catalyze shifts in business models, creating new threats and opportunities for incumbent interests.

Understand Technology

Most technology companies spend around 5 percent of their sales on R&D. Media companies spend almost nothing. However, technology now represents not only a channel but for many the future, or at least a good portion of their future. It is essential that companies understand the technologies that will drive their businesses in the future. This is made more imperative as the forces such as digitization blur the distinctions that used to separate technologies and even industries. A world in which Google, HP, Intel, Microsoft, and YouTube are most interested in moving from the office and into the living room presents myriad threats and opportunities for complementors.

Serve the Consumers' Needs (Do Not Serve Them Subpoenas)

Suing your potential customers is a terrible idea. This cannot be stressed strongly enough. The RIAA compares the people it sues to shoplifters (thinking "pirate" too glamorous a word), and they have a point. These people are stealing. But the vacuum that existed that allowed the creation of such rampant shoplifting is a function of the atomization of content enabled by the convergence of technology forces and the absence of a compelling legal alternative. Suing consumers gives the content industry the appearance of meaningful action, but does nothing to address the underlying causes.

CONCLUSION

The technologies discussed in this book change what it means to create, distribute, and consume entertainment. In some ways we have been here before, but today's forces are turbocharged compared to what came in the past. As we have seen, value was created as technology provided new channels for existing content, for example as television and VCRs breathed new life into old movies. Today's forces can create value but they can also destroy value for incumbents.

The best thing that executives in the content and technology industries can do is better understand these forces and better understand each other. The worst thing content company executives can do is look to Congress to apply misconceived legislation to lock into amber unbalanced IP laws that ignore the power and potential for value creation of new technologies and content. The worse thing that technology company executives can do is try to capture lock-in at the expense of a robust consumer experience. Too many people have seen the "Wintel" movie to allow lock-in to happen without a big fight. And in the meantime we all suffer from wasteful standards battles.

In this very dynamic time only one thing is certain: nothing will be the same for entertainment and technology industries. That could be good for them and us.

APPENDIX A: THE FORCES SHAPING
THE FUTURE OF ENTERTAINMENT

TECHNOLOGIES USUALLY DRIVE toward increased consumer convenience (difficulties with actually programming your VCR notwithstanding, especially when attached to a cable set-top box). But today things are different. We live at the confluence of several technological forces, independent but related, that fundamentally change the outlook for the usual suspects. These forces offer tremendous opportunities and risks.

Following is a brief discussion of the most relevant forces having an impact on the future of entertainment. We often hear about these forces, such as Moore's Law, but many of us are uncertain what they really mean or how they affect us. If you are curious, read on.

MOORE'S LAW

The first force to consider is Moore's Law. The phrase gets used often and is often misused. In general, Moore's Law describes the large increase (doubling) in the processing power of computers every year or so. This phenomenon was first described by Gordon E. Moore, the cofounder of microchip giant Intel. Moore observed that the number of transistors that microchip (more generally known as semiconductor) manufacturers were able to fit on an integrated circuit doubled every twelve to eighteen months and predicted the continuation of this exponential growth in the article titled "Cramming More Components onto Integrated Circuits" in *Electronics,* April 19, 1965. It is difficult to really comprehend the size of the increase in transistors over time described by Moore's Law. Moore used to compare the number of transistors produced by the semiconductor industry in a year to the number of ants crawling on the earth, a figure that Moore cites Harvard entomologist E. O. Wilson as estimating at between ten to the sixteenth and ten to the seventeenth powers. By early 2003, due to the relentless growth described by his law, Moore was look-ing for a new metaphor to describe the number of transistors produced by the industry in a year. By then, the industry was producing ten to the eighteenth (1,000,000,000,000,000,000) or one quintillion transistors in a year: enough so that each ant would have to carry ten to the one hundredth transistors. As the number of transistors produced each year increased, their costs declined. By early 2003, a consumer could buy fifty million transistors on a lower-end microchip for a dollar.[1] The impact of Moore's Law was projected presciently in a cartoon in that 1965 article that depicted "Handy Home Computers" be-ing sold next to notions and cosmetics in a department store. That is close to what Moore's Law predicted.

Microprocessors (such as the Intel Pentium or Dual Core chip) are the "brains," or perhaps more precisely, "cerebral cortex" of the computer. These chips are far more complex and expensive than the low-end (DRAM) chips costing a dollar that Gordon Moore described in 2003. Microprocessors and software, such as the PC's operating systems (for example, Windows XP) and applications (programs such as Microsoft Word), are the most valuable parts of the PC. The rest is basically a commodity, like soy beans or pork bellies, all pretty much the same. Technology following the path described by Moore's Law has led to increasingly powerful personal computers being introduced every year. This relentless cycle has led to regular reductions in the prices of computers. Now, consumers can buy computers for around $500 that are as powerful as computers that would have cost $2,000 just five years earlier.

NETWORKING

Computers connect to other computers through a network. Networks can connect two computers in your home, or thousands of computers in a com-pany. Networks can even connect millions of computers to each other. One famous network is the Internet. The Internet is a worldwide system of com-puter networks—a network of networks in which users at any one computer (or node) can, if they have permission, get information from any other com-puter. The Internet was conceived by the Advanced Research Projects Agency (ARPA) of the U.S. government in 1969. The original aim was to create a net-work that would allow users of research computers at one university to be able to communicate with research computers at other universities. An important feature of its design was its robustness; because messages could be routed or rerouted in more than one direction, the network could continue to function even if parts of it were destroyed. This feature was originally a function of the Internet's early sponsor, the U.S. military. They wanted their computers to be able to communicate even if some of the nodes along the network were wiped out, for example, in a nuclear war.

The most widely used part of the Internet is the World Wide Web (the www that you type in when you enter an Internet address). The WWW is the entire universe of resources and people on the Internet using Hypertext Transfer Protocol (HTTP), a set of rules devised by British researcher Tim Berners-Lee working at the European physics research center, CERN, in the early 1990s. Through the Web, users have easy access to millions of pages of information. Web usage greatly increased after 1993, when a program called Mosaic was released by the National Center for Supercomputing Applications (NCSA) at the University of Illinois in Urbana, Illinois. Mosaic was the first widely distributed graphical browser, or viewer, for the World Wide Web. Like the browsers that followed it, Mosaic was a client program that used HTTP to make requests of Web servers throughout the Internet on behalf of the browser user. Once Mosaic was available, and was closely followed by its corporate cousin, the Netscape Navigator browser (which has long since been supplanted by Microsoft's browser, Explorer), the Web virtually exploded in numbers of users and content sites.

The explosion in popularity of the Web and concomitant increase in Web content created fertile markets for search engines and portals such as Yahoo! and others that collected, sorted, and organized the fast-increasing content of the Web. These companies had few assets other than talented designers and engineers and increasingly powerful servers. The popular and financial successes of high-profile search engines and portals demonstrated the power of the client-server business model applied to the Internet.

CLIENT-SERVER COMPUTING

Client-server describes the relationship between two computer programs in which one program, the client, makes a service request from another program, the server, which fulfills the request. In everyday terms, your PC is a client, and whenever you check your e-mail you are making a service request of your e-mail provider's server. In a network, the client-server model provides a convenient way to interconnect programs that are distributed efficiently across different locations. The client-server model became one of the central ideas of network computing. A prominent example of a client-server struc-ture is the Internet's main program, TCP/IP (transmission control protocol/ Internet protocol). Relative to the Internet, a Web browser is a client program that requests services (for example, the sending of Web pages or files) from a Web server (which technically is called an HTTP or HTTP server) in another computer somewhere on the Internet. Similarly, a computer with TCP/IP in-stalled makes client requests for files from file transfer protocol (FTP) servers in other computers on the Internet.

MP3 TECHNOLOGY

Another important force was the emergence of a digital compression format for music called "MP3." This is an abbreviation for "MPEG-1, Level 3." MPEG standards are created by the Moving Picture Experts Group (MPEG), a group of scientists and industry representatives working with the International Or-ganization for Standardization (ISO).[2] What made MP3 immediately com-pelling was that with MP3 one could compress a music file (in other words, a song) from a CD to about a tenth of its size. In comparison, most digital audio and video files were very large and memory-intensive and therefore un-wieldy for storage or transport. MP3 was originally created by a partnership between the consumer electronics company Thomson Multimedia, owner of the RCA brand, and the German Fraunhoffer Institute under the aegis of MPEG. These companies' role in creating MP3 appeared to be no different than, say, Sony or Microsoft's ongoing initiatives to create new formats, or Philips' creation of the CD about twenty-five years earlier. However, the key difference between MP3 and digital formats created by Sony or Microsoft was that MP3 was licensed early and cheaply by the ISO. Therefore, the fact that the ISO is a nonprofit organization committed to promoting standardiza-tion worldwide has been pivotal in making MP3 the ubiquitous standard for digital music.

The process of creating an MP3 file by copying music from a CD is very easy. This is done through a process called "ripping." Consumers can convert CD music into MP3 files in short order; it takes less than ten minutes for a consumer to rip a full-length CD into MP3 files. These files can then be played on the user's PC, e-mailed to friends, or distributed on the Internet.

That is what all those Napster users were doing. Because the files are digitally encoded, it is possible to produce MP3 files with no loss in audio quality no matter how many times the file is copied.

PEER-TO-PEER TECHNOLOGY

The phrase "peer-to-peer" (often abbreviated P-to-P, or P2P) refers to a set of technologies that enables the direct exchange of services or data between any groups of computers. Using P-to-P technology, some or all of the resources of any group of computers—such as processing cycles, cache storage, and disc storage for files—could be harnessed and directed. P-to-P technology enables enterprises to take advantage of distributed computing resources—their own, or others'—by enabling a direct exchange of services between computers. There are two flavors of P-to-P systems: hybrid and pure. Hybrid P-to-P systems use a central computer or group of computers (servers) to route requests that users make from their clients (PCs). When a Napster user searched the service for a song title, the Napster servers searched all of the clients that were connected to Napster at that moment and returned the options, telling the user matches it found and the estimated time it would take to transmit a copy to the user's computer. Napster had one thing going for it: it had millions of users. It had two things going against it: it was located in the United States and subject to U.S. law, and it used a hybrid P-to-P system. Unplug the server and you unplug Napster. The filesharing companies that sprang up in the wake of Napster are pure P-to-P services; they do not rely on a central server. In addition, the most popular service today, KaZaa, is domiciled outside of the United States. Thus the recording companies have resorted to suing KaZaa's users, that little girl and grandmother in Chapter 1 among several hundred, because they were powerless to do much directly to the company itself, at least by going through U.S. courts.

BROADBAND

Broadband describes various technologies that transfer data bits (whether they form an e-mail message, picture, spreadsheet, movie, phone call, or so on) at speeds far greater than possible by ordinary dial-up modems. Many broadband technologies currently available enable users to download at speeds exceeding a million bits per second. The power of broadband lies in the potential for new applications and services that are made possible by the transfer of information (bits) at such high speeds.

Broadband technologies also promised to change the economics and usage patterns of consumer Web access. Many Internet service providers (ISPs) offer unlimited use (flat rate) pricing packages. This was a boon in the United States, where most consumers were not directly charged for local calls and dialed into a local ISP phone number to access the Internet. When ISP AOL changed to flat-rate access in the United States in December 1996, usage increased to seventy minutes per day from fourteen minutes per day prior to all-you-can-eat pricing. In Europe, AOL and other ISPs have also moved to flat-rate pricing; however, local calls are often still metered in many European countries, inhibiting Internet usage. Regardless of call pricing policies, most consumers access the Internet via traditional phone lines, alternating between surfing the Web and using their (single) phone line for voice calls. If you are surfing the Web, you cannot be on the phone, and vice versa. By contrast, broadband technologies do not interfere with a consumer's phone (voice) connection and thus can be left engaged—"always on" in the parlance.

There are several methods currently available to deliver broadband to homes. In general, they provide bandwidth through standard telephone lines (copper wire twisted pair) already installed in homes, through cable TV coaxial cable, or via satellite. Each of these modes was originally designed for another purpose, for example, voice telephone service or transmission of television signals. In the 1980s and 1990s, engineers began trying a variety of approaches to connect homes for high-speed data communications. This industry note describes three of them. The first two—broadband over cable TV lines and over phone lines—use clever technologies to wring the most out of existing wires to the home: hybrid fiber-coax makes use of the cable TV industry's infrastructure, which includes fiberoptic lines in addition to coaxial cable; the digital subscriber line (DSL), meanwhile, exploits frequencies much higher than those used to convey conversations to send high-speed data over pairs of copper telephone wires. Cable and DSL were by far the two leading technologies for delivering broadband to the home. Among the most economically developed nations in the world, the members of the Organization for Economic Cooperation and Development, cable led DSL in consumer broadband penetration. In 1999, 84 percent of consumer broadband subscribers used cable versus 16 percent with DSL. By the end of 2000, cable had slipped to 55 percent versus 45 percent with DSL. By June 2001, cable had edged out DSL by 51 percent to 49 percent.[3] The proportions in the United States were somewhat different.

Cable television systems have emerged as the early leader in providing such high-speed data access in the home. Currently, cable accounts for 70 percent of consumer broadband in the United States. A cable television system is a company that lays and services coaxial cable and presents programming that is transmitted through the coaxial cable that runs into subscribers' homes and screws into their TVs or set-top boxes.[4] Cable television system operators are distinct from cable networks, which provide programming. However, some multiple systems operators, or their parent companies, also own cable networks.

The same coaxial cable that runs into each cable subscriber's home is capable of delivering broadband Internet access (and telephone service too). To access the Internet, the subscriber must have a cable modem, a device that attaches to the cable just like a TV converter box but decodes and manipulates data rather than television signals. Beginning in the late 1980s, many cable companies began upgrading their networks with high-capacity fiberoptics to support delivery of enhanced, two-way services such as interactive television—which did not win broad consumer support—and video on demand (pay per view), which fared better. Broadband Internet access offered a new, rich market for this transmission capacity. By the mid-1990s, some cable companies had introduced broadband Internet services for their subscribers. The hybrid fiber-coax (HFC) systems that cable companies laid with an eye to offering interactive TV and pay-per-view services offered consumers very large capacity for bit transmission. Just one of the many television channels offered to subscribers can carry almost 30 megabits per second (mbs) to the home.[5]

High-capacity optical fibers connect the cable operator's central facility (the "head end") to each neighborhood area (the "node"), which typically encompasses about a thousand homes, each a potential customer. In an HFC system, the data channel is shared among the homes linked by coax to the end of the local fiberoptic line. Thus the actual data rate achieved in any individual home depends on the number of users sharing the channel at a given time.[6] Most cable broadband customers experience speeds of 1 mbs. There is also a lower-speed channel in the reverse direction to carry data from the home back to the Internet.

Cable operators stole a march on the telecommunications companies by offering broadband Internet access to consumers almost two years earlier than most regional Bell operating companies (RBOCs). Between the passage of the Telecommunications Act of 1996 and early 2001, the cable industry spent $42 billion to deploy broadband infrastructure in order to offer various advanced services such as high-speed Internet access, digital music, and telephony. In March 2001, U.S. cable companies gained their four millionth consumer broadband customer, double the number of broadband customers they had by the end of 1999. The success of the cable companies is credited with spurring telephone companies to offer their own consumer broadband services.

Currently, most broadband over telephone lines uses a variety of DSL technologies, which taken together are often abbreviated as "xDSL."[7] By the beginning of 2002, around 28 percent of all broadband subscribers in the United States used some version of DSL.

In the United States, DSL service was provided by RBOCs and competitive local exchange carriers (CLECs). In 2000, four of the leading five DSL providers were RBOCs.

The capacity of a communications channel depends on its bandwidth (the range of frequencies it can use) and its signal-to-noise ratio (which depends on the quality of the connection). In 1948, a Bell Labs scientist, Claude E. Shannon, calculated the theoretical transmission capacity of telephone lines at about 35 kbs. It took thirty years of modem development to attain that speed. Modems operating at 56 kbs achieve such rates by taking advantage of digital connections that circumvent some sources of noise in transmissions toward the end user.[8] These modems are still limited to upload (signals sent toward the ISP) rates of 33.6 kbs.

There are several ways currently available to transmit data at high rates over the twisted pair of copper wires designed to convey phone calls and in place in almost every home in the United States. A technology known as integrated services digital network (ISDN), which transmits data at up to 128 kbs, had been gaining popularity since the mid-1990s. Much faster transmission speeds, operating at 1.544 mbs, have been available from T1 lines, initially developed to enable multiple-voice connections using a single line. T1 has traditionally been priced for commercial voice access, which is much more costly and more than most people can afford for data access.

The twisted pair of copper telephone wires from a home typically runs to the local exchange carrier's central office containing a switch. A switch is a complex piece of equipment that routes telephone calls to other switches or phones as necessary. DSL service does not use the existing switching equip-ment. DSL switches are installed in the central office to exploit the full data-carrying capacity of the wires, which normal phone calls do not use. This allows DSL subscribers to simultaneously use the same twisted-pair wires for telephone calls and data transmission. Most DSL technologies use a signal splitter installed at the subscriber's premises. Installation of the splitter re-quires a phone company technician visit, which adds to the startup costs of the service.

At present, DSL services can be provided to homes within a four- to five-kilometer radius from the telecommunication exchange or central office. The most widely deployed version is asymmetric DSL, or ADSL. It is capable of de-livering 3 to 4 mbs to the home and a slower rate back from the home, typically a small fraction of a megabit per second. However, in practice, DSL users in the United States experience the Internet at a lugubrious rate of .6 mbs or so.

APPENDIX B: TOOLS OF RESISTANCE: PATENTS AND COPYRIGHTS

TODAY WHEN INCUMBENT COMPANIES are worried about new challengers, they often look to use intellectual property (IP) laws as a kind of bludgeon. IP rights are important tools for promoting innovation. Patents, copyrights, and trademarks can be valuable property rights that help creators and innovators earn a return from their work. Patents and copyrights in particular, when used wisely, can also help a technology or piece of content march through the Ascension stage and into Prosperity. However, today the extension of IP rights is controversial and much in the news. Opponents of issues such as copyright extensions and more liberal patenting cite the damaging effects these actions have on innovation. This appendix is a brief primer on IP as it pertains to the content and technologies discussed in this book.

The specific form of intellectual property determines the type of legal protection it can receive. Novel inventions or processes can qualify for patent protection; movies and recordings usually qualify for copyrights (trade names, logos, and commercial designs are protected by trademarks). These properties can be very important to their owners. In 1998, patent licensing revenues exceeded $100 billion around the world.[1] According to a trade group, copyright industries in the United States (book and music publishing, film production, radio and television broadcasting, and computer software development) accounted for $535.1 billion, or 5.24 percent of the United States gross domestic product and achieved estimated foreign sales and exports of $88.97 billion in 2001.[2]

In the United States, the monopoly rights generated by patents have provoked a certain amount of ambivalence. Much of this ambivalence was epitomized by Thomas Jefferson, who, prior to becoming the third president of the United States, had been the first head of the United States Patent Office. Jefferson had once been philosophically opposed to the idea of patents, considering them to be unfair monopolies. However, his views changed somewhat as he recognized the potential for patents to spur creativity. Jefferson wrote, "He who receives an idea from me, receives instruction himself without lessening mine; as he who lights his taper at mine, receives light without darkening me." But Jefferson added, "Society may give an exclusive right to the profits arising from them, as an encouragement to men to pursue ideas which may produce utility, but this may or may not be done, according to the will and convenience of the society, without claim or complaint from anybody.[3]

Society was meant to be the main beneficiary of the inventiveness that patents were designed to catalyze. Patents, copyrights, and other vehicles of IP protection recognize a balance between the needs of society and the needs of inventors and creators. The limitations placed on these vehicles (such as time limits, concepts of fair use, and so on) are the fulcrum upon which these needs are balanced.

Since the 1950s, both the United States Patent and Trademark Office (USPTO) and Congress have increasingly expanded (and courts have upheld) the range of discoveries subject to patent protection. This increase in the types of innovations that were patent-eligible sparked controversy, especially in recent years as companies successfully patented certain business processes, which hitherto had not been considered eligible for patent. Similarly, the terms of copyright protection have recently been greatly expanded. Critics of these extensions argued that they reduced the public domain to the benefit of corporate interests against those of the public.

The broadening of the scope of patent-eligible innovations and the increase in the terms of copyright protection put under a spotlight the question of who is meant to benefit from IP protection. The concept of using IP rights to promote innovation is well accepted in the United States. However, these actions have promoted discord, because some believe that they are unfair or even inimical to promoting innovation. Some software firms complained that recent broad patent awards made innovation more difficult because they must avoid (or license) patented subprocesses that would be components of new software programs. Others pointed to extended copyright terms as stifling creativity and development, as material that would be in the public domain remained protected. Legal scholar Paul Goldstein compared lawmakers' attitudes to copyright protections over time as "viewing a glass as half empty or half full," where the emphasis on protection varyingly tilted toward the public domain or private interests.[4] For the past ten years many large and important industries, even those that are complementors such as movie studios and computer companies, felt they had divergent interests in how Congress and the courts viewed the glass.

The key principle governing patent protection is that the inventor receives a government-mandated right to control the patented invention in exchange for disclosing the elements of the invention. In general in the United States, the first inventor of a claimed invention has the sole right to file for and receive a patent. To preserve rights to acquire a United States patent, the inventor must file a patent application with the USPTO within one year of the first date on which the invention was in public use or available for sale.

In all cases, it was up to the patent holder to enforce a patent. The Patent and Trademark Office only issues patents; enforcement was typically handled in the courts. It can cost hundreds of thousands to several millions of dollars to defend a patent in court.

Although patents offer well-defined advantages, they are not always the best vehicle used to protect IP. Patents offer monopoly protection for a finite period of time. Other forms of IP, such as copyright, offer protection for longer periods of time, while trade secrets offer protection indefinitely.

Although patents and copyrights can sometimes be used to protect the same piece of IP, they are very different vehicles and serve different purposes. A patent for an invention is the grant of a monopoly property right to the inventor, issued by the USPTO. The term of a new patent is twenty years from the date on which the application for the patent (or the provisional application) was filed in the United States. United States patent grants are effective only within the United States, U.S. territories, and U.S. possessions. Patents are registered with the USPTO.

Copyright is a form of protection provided to the creators (or their employers in cases of "works for hire") of "original works of authorship"; which can include literary, dramatic, musical, artistic, and many other works, both published and unpublished. The 1976 Copyright Act generally gives the owner of a copyright the exclusive right to reproduce the copyrighted work, to prepare derivative works, to distribute copies of the copyrighted work, to perform the copyrighted work publicly, or to display the copyrighted work publicly. Copyrights are registered by the Copyright Office of the Library of Congress.

A patent offers limited monopoly property rights to inventions that successfully meet the requirements for patent. Most of the recent controversy surrounding patents has been over the increased scope of patent-eligible innovations, mostly relating to software and process patents. Some critics accuse the USPTO of failing to understand the true nature of software or software-based processes and issuing patents for processes that are too broad. These critics say such patents actually inhibit innovation because they produce a tangle of patented processes that are difficult to innovate around.

Copyright protects the form of expression rather than the subject matter. Thus Mickey Mouse is copyrighted, but the idea of a comic mouse is not copyrightable. A great deal of controversy has surrounded recent legislative action extending the terms of copyright in the United States. Congress has extended copyright terms for new and existing works eleven times in the past forty years. Critics contend that these extensions ultimately reduce innovation in order to expand the property interests of copyright holders, and point with irony to the fact that Disney, a major lobbyer for the 1998 Copyright Extension Act, enjoyed much early success by parodying or outright appropriating copyrighted stories (in a less-litigious time in the 1920s) or those that had fallen into the public domain. Under the 1998 Copyright Extension Act (sometimes referred to as the Mickey Mouse Copyright Extension Act, or the Sonny Bono act), Disney's characters (among many other copyrighted expressions) would enjoy greatly prolonged protection, with the result that copyright extensions now protect Disney's characters from the same appropriation that the company practiced in its earlier history.

PATENTS

A patent grants an inventor the right to exclude others from producing or using the inventor's discovery or invention for a set period of time. In exchange for the right to exclude others from using, making, or selling the invention, an inventor discloses the details of the patented invention. Once issued, patents become public record. Failure to disclose the details concerning the invention can result in an invalid patent. In the United States, patent laws were enacted by Congress under the Constitution, "To promote the progress of science and useful arts, by securing for limited times to authors and inventors the exclusive right to their respective writings and discoveries."[5]

To be patented, an invention must be novel, useful, and not of an obvious nature. The United States Patent and Trademark Office, the federal agency charged with administering patent laws, will not grant a patent on an invention that was publicly used or available for sale by anyone, including the inventor, more than one year before the inventor filed a patent application. Identical or similar inventions that others publicly disclose anywhere in the world before an inventor files a patent application, known as "prior art," may prevent the inventor from obtaining patent protection because the invention would not be considered novel.

Not everything under the sun can be patented. Abstract ideas, mental processes, laws of nature, and physical phenomena are exempt from patent. For example, Charles Darwin could not have patented his theory of evolution, and Albert Einstein did not need to bother the patent office with his formula for the theory of relativity; nor could a mineral or plant found in the wild be patented. Literary, dramatic, musical, or artistic works cannot be patented, but are usually subject to copyright protection.

From the time of the Founding Fathers until recently, patents were normally issued for a nonrenewable period of seventeen years, beginning from the date of issuance. Under a 1995 change prompted by the Agreement on Trade-Related Aspects of Intellectual Property accompanying the Uruguay Round of the General Agreement on Tariffs and Trade, patent terms were extended to twenty years measured from the date of application.

Each patent application for a new invention is reviewed by an examiner to determine whether it is entitled to a patent. In the past a model was required as part of a patent application; in most cases today, only a detailed specification is necessary.[6] If an application is rejected, the decision may be appealed to the Patent Office's Board of Appeals, with further or alternative review available from the United States Court of Appeals for the Federal Circuit, or the United States District Court for the District of Columbia, and onward to the United States Supreme Court.

An issued patent can be overturned if prior art exists that demonstrates an invention was not novel or was obvious at the time the patent application was filed. For example, journals or trade publications that describe aspects of the patented invention may be sufficient to establish prior art and thus invalidate a patent.

In latter years, some software developers and other enterprises have sought and been awarded business-method patents on software. Such patents prevent others from creating, using, or selling a program that performs the same process or function as the patented program, even if different underlying code is used. Many of these business-method patents are controversial because they give patent protection to business processes, such as reverse auctions over the

Internet (eBay) or easy "1-click" online purchase processes (Amazon.com), that critics contend are not novel.

Patent fees can represent a substantial source of revenue for their owners and a substantial cost for manufacturers. For a sub-$30 DVD player, patent fees are the most expensive single component, accounting for $6–$12 of the manufacturing cost. Dolby audio makes a few cents per unit. The remote control device costs as little as $1.50–$2.00. The disc mechanism and circuits cost $4–$5 for everything including the drive motor. The optical pickup costs about $2–$3 if purchased in large quantities; a few dollars more if purchased in bulk amounts under 100,000. Tool unit cost for production runs over 300,000 units is about $1.[7]

COPYRIGHT[8]

Compared with patents, copyright offers a less restrictive but far longer-lasting form of IP protection. Copyright protects the particular way in which a work, such as a poem, movie, or computer program, is expressed. Of the various forms of IP protection, none have proved as contentious over the past hundred years as copyright. Legal scholars, as well as businesses, realize that decisions concerning the scope and length of copyright protection are extraordinarily influential and have an impact on the quantity, quality, and cost of future content.[9] The current battle over copyright places the interests of technology producers, such as PC makers, against those of copyright holders, content producers such as recording companies and movie studios. This tension stretches back into the early 20th century.

Blatant copyright infringement is as old as copyright protection itself. Sometimes infringement was sanctioned, tacitly or overtly, by governments. When it was a developing country (and even after it had become economically well-developed), the United States refused to recognize the copyrights of non-U.S. citizens. Foreign copyright holders, such as authors and composers, chaffed at the rampant piracy of their works in the United States. The author Charles Dickens, on his American lecture tours, was a vocal critic of the fact that his copyrights were not recognized in this country. The composer Sir Arthur Sullivan (of Gilbert and Sullivan) even went so far as to copyright some of his compositions under the names of United States citizens who in turn remitted to Sullivan royalties from this country.[10] Then as now, music was at the forefront of the tension between content owners and technology companies.

Copyright protects only physical representation of a given work and not the ideas, concepts, procedures, processes, or methods of operation that may underlie that representation. For example, as noted earlier, although Disney's Mickey Mouse is protected by copyright (and other legal devices), the idea itself of a fun-loving rodent is not subject to copyright. In *NEC Corp.* v. *Intel Corp.*, in which NEC sought to have Intel's copyrights on its 8086 and 8088 microcodes invalidated, and in which Intel countersued for copyright infringement, a court found that microcodes (instructions that perform specific processing functions and are not program-addressable) can be copyrighted, but alternative microcodes that are not substantially similar, even though some of their subroutines may be similar because their underlying ideas were straightforward and capable of only a limited range of expression, do not infringe.[11] Thus, Intel's microcodes were proper subject matter for copyright, but NEC did not infringe such rights because its microcodes were not substantially similar. A copyright owner has the right to prevent others from making unauthorized, literal copies of the copyrighted work, but not from independently creating works that may tell similar stories, in the case of novels or movies, or perform the same functions, in the case of software. Thus while the pioneering spreadsheet program Visicalc enjoyed copyright protection, others were free to develop software that performed similar functions.

To be copyrightable, a work must be "fixed" or recorded in some format and must be original, that is, independently created by its author. Copyright protection begins as soon as an original work is fixed in a tangible medium of expression. Creators may register their work with the United States Copyright Office, but that is not necessary to obtain full copyright protection. A work does not need to be novel (that is, formerly unknown) or even lawful to be protected by copyright. For example, the fact that a federal judge found the filesharing service Napster unlawful did not in any way invalidate the copyright that Napster enjoyed on its software. In fact, even obscene works can enjoy copyright protection.[12]

A copyright is ordinarily awarded to the creator or creators of a work for the life of the copyright. In the United States, beginning with the first Copyright Act in 1790, the initial terms of copyright were set at a term of 14 years. The 1790 Act also provided that, if the author survived the initial term, he or his executors, administrators, or assigns could renew the copyright for another term of 14 years. Subsequent copyright acts expanded the terms of protection. In response to copyright extensions enacted in England,

Congress passed the Copyright Act of 1831, which increased the copyright term to 28 years, with renewal available for an additional 14 years, matching the copyright extension granted by Parliament. In response to these actions, France extended its copyright terms to the life of the author plus 50 years, Russia extended its copyright term to life of the author plus 20 years, and perpetual rights were granted in Germany, Norway, and Sweden. In 1909, Congress expanded the initial copyright period to 28 years and increased the renewal term to 28 years.

After a series of brief extensions in the first half of the twentieth century, Congress passed the Copyright Act of 1976, enacting a term of life of the author plus 50 years for works created or published after January 1, 1978. This made United States copyright terms congruent with the Berne Convention for the Protection of Literary and Artistic Works, an international copyright treaty begun in 1886 and which the United States joined in 1989. Today both American and European copyrights, under the auspices of the Berne Convention, run for 70 years beyond the life of the author. For "works made for hire," the copyright endures for a term of 95 years from the year of its first publication, or a term of 120 years from the year of its creation, whichever expires first.[13]

Software was subject to copyright protection in the United States after Congress passed the 1976 Copyright Act. Prior to this act, there had been uncertainty whether copyright law could protect software. This uncertainty stemmed from the fact that functional instructions and ideas—the heart of a computer program—are not copyrightable because they do not meet the minimal copyright requirement for creativity. Court decisions since the 1980s and congressional guidance led to the inclusion of computer programs and databases under copyright law.

When a copyright is awarded, the author is given a temporary monopoly in original creation. This monopoly takes the form of six rights in areas where the author retains exclusive control. These rights are

1. Right of reproduction (copying)
2. Right to create derivative works
3. Right of distribution
4. Right of performance
5. Right to display
6. Right of digital transmission

Copyright protects the first two rights in both private and public contexts, whereas an author can restrict the last four rights only in the public sphere.[14] Any violations of these property rights are considered copyright infringement.

There are limitations to the property rights conveyed by copyright. The most prominent exception falls under "fair use." The doctrine of fair use allows the reproduction and use of copyrighted material for purposes such as criticism, parody, and news reporting as well as teaching and research.[15] The boundaries of fair use have been frequently challenged in court, and since it has had a fluid definition, subject to judicial interpretation, the concept of fair use can be a thin reed for consumers, offering uncertain protection. Another limitation is the first sale doctrine. Under this provision, ownership of a physical copy of a copyrighted work, such as a book or record, permits a range of activities such as lending the item, reselling the item, disposing of the item, destroying the item, and so forth, but it does not permit copying the item in its entirety. That is because the transfer of the physical copy does not include transfer of the copyright to the work. This doctrine will be challenged by proposed legislation intended to fight piracy in an era when perfect digital copies of copyrighted works are easily made and distributed.

Conflicting patent and copyright claims are open to judicial resolution. However, claims of infringement, or disputes about rightful ownership of IP, are costly and time-consuming to resolve. According to a 2001 survey conducted by the American Intellectual Property Lawyer's Association, a patent litigant can expect to spend at least $500,000 and up to $6 million to try a patent case. On average, a patent suit in which $1 million to $25 million is at risk costs $797,000 through discovery, and just under $1.5 million through trial, with some litigants reporting costs in excess of $2.5 million. For those cases in which more than $25 million is at risk, the average litigant can expect to spend $1.5 million through discovery and roughly $3 million if there is a trial. Many small companies cannot afford the money or time needed to fight a dispute.

Although some patents have been controversial (for example, business method or process patents) and left to the courts to decide, copyright issues over the years have been fraught with contention. The Supreme Court has weighed in on a number of copyright conflicts involving content producers. The Court has delivered numerous opinions that interpret a consistent view of the purpose of copyright. In 1932, the Court wrote, "The sole interest of the

United States and the primary object in conferring the monopoly lie in the general benefits derived by the public from the labors of authors."[16] In 1948, the Court wrote, "The copyright law, like the patent statutes, makes reward to the owner a secondary consideration."[17]

In the 1984 Betamax case the Court wrote, "The primary objective of copyright is not to reward the labor of authors but to promote the Progress of Science and useful Arts."[18] However, it is within the purview of Congress to decide the term (length) of copyright protection.

Since 1962, Congress extended the term of copyright protection eleven times. Copyright scholar Paul Goldstein of Stanford Law School has written, "[T]he U.S. Congress has been far more consistent in extending rights against economically valuable uses than a strict showing of needed incentives would appear to indicate. . . . Congress has never once required authors or publishers to demonstrate that, in fact, they need the new right as an incentive to produce literary or artistic works."[19]

NOTES

Chapter 1

1. Amy Harmon, "Piracy, or Innovation? It's Hollywood vs. High Tech," *The New York Times,* March 14, 2002.

2. In 1980, home video accounted for only an estimated 7 percent of studio revenue. This grew to 40 percent by 2000. Source: Harold L. Vogel, *Entertainment Industry Economics* (Cambridge: Cambridge University Press, 2001) p. 62, table 2.8. By 2006, home video accounted for 60 percent of domestic revenues for U.S. studios. Source: Video Software Dealers Association. [www.idealink.org/resource.Phx/USDA/pressroom/quick-facts.htm].

3. Carl Shapiro and Hal R. Varian, *Information Rules* (Boston: Harvard Business School Press, 1999), p. 3.

4. Jennifer Ordonez, "Behind the Music: MCA Spent Millions on Carly Hennessy," *Wall Street Journal,* February 26, 2002, A-1.

5. William Hellmuth Jr., "The Motion Picture Industry," in *The Structure of American Industry,* 3rd ed., ed. Walter Adams (New York: Macmillan, 1961), p. 395.

6. Robert W. Crandall and Charles L. Jackson, "The $500 Billion Opportunity: The Potential Economic Benefit of Widespread Diffusion of Broadband Internet Access," The Brookings Institution, July 2001. [www.criterioneconomics.com/documents/Crandall_Jackson_500_Billion_Opportunity_July_2001.pdf]. The authors conclude that universal adoption of broadband in the United States ("universal" defined as equal to the 94 percent of U.S. households with at least one phone line) could provide consumers with economic benefits of up to $400 billion per year, while producers of network equipment, household computers, ancillary equipment, and software and producers and distributors of entertainment products could benefit by as much as $100 billion per year (p. 2). It should be noted that this study was commissioned by the New York-based RBOC Verizon.

7. Source of the 2001 figure is Michael Pastore, "New Records Predicted for Holiday E-Commerce," *E-Commerce News,* October 21, 2001; source of the 2005 figure is Jupiter Research.

8. P. William Bane and Stephen P. Bradley, "The Light at the End of the Pipe," *Scientific American,* October 1999, 110–115.

9. Pew Internet & American Life Project, May 2005 Survey.

Chapter 2

1. Alvin F. Harlow, *Old Wires and New Waves* (New York: D. Appleton-Century Company, 1936), pp. 455–456.

2. Ray Stannard Baker, "Marconi's Achievement," *McClure's Magazine,* February 1902, *18,* 291.

3. Degna Marconi, *My Father, Marconi* (New York: McGraw Hill, 1962), p. 12.

4. Marconi, *My Father, Marconi,* p. 15.

5. Source: the very interesting and handy purchasing power calculator provided online by Economic History Services, www.eh.net. All subsequent comparisons of purchasing power come from this source.

6. Barnouw, *A Tower in Babel: A History of Broadcasting in the United States, Vol. I—to 1933* (New York: Oxford University Press, 1966), p. 12.

7. H.J.W. Dam, "Telegraphing Without Wires," *McClure's Magazine,* March 1897, *8*(5), 383–392.

8. W. J. Baker, *A History of the Marconi Company* (London: Metheun and Company, 1970), p. 85.

9. Susan J. Douglas, *Inventing American Broadcasting: 1899–1922* (Baltimore: Johns Hopkins University Press, 1988), p. 40.

10. Ray Stannard Baker, "Marconi's Achievement," p. 298.

11. Ray Stannard Baker, "Marconi's Achievement," p. 299.

12. Douglas, *Inventing American Broadcasting,* p. 71.

13. As University of Michigan Professor of Communications Susan J. Douglas has observed, "The company hoped that its nonintercommunication policy would somewhat compensate for its decision not to sue infringers at that time (1904)." Douglas, *Inventing American Broadcasting,* p. 72.

14. Douglas, *Inventing American Broadcasting,* p. 72.

15. Douglas, *Inventing American Broadcasting,* p. 73.

16. Douglas, *Inventing American Broadcasting,* p. 40.

17. Barnouw, *A Tower in Babel,* p. 21.

18. Barnouw, *A Tower in Babel,* p. 22.

19. Barnouw, *A Tower in Babel,* p. 23.

20. Tom Lewis, *Empire of the Air* (New York: Edward Burlingame Books, 1991), p. 80.

21. *New York Times,* February 14, 1909, p. 1. Cited in Douglas, *Inventing American Broadcasting,* p. 172.

22. Lewis, *Empire of the Air,* p. 85.

23. Barnouw, *A Tower in Babel,* p. 45.

24. *Marconi v. De Forest,* 236 Fed.942.

25. Allen Koenigsberg, "The Birth of the Recording Industry." Adapted from "The Seventeen-Year Itch," an address delivered at the U.S. Patent Office Bi-Centennial in Washington, D.C., on May 9, 1990. [http://members.aol.com/allenamet/BirthRec.htm].

26. Thomas A. Edison, "The Phonograph and Its Future," The North American Review, May 1878, *126*(262).

27. "The History of the Edison Cylinder," The United States Library of Congress [http://memory.loc.gov/ammem/edhtml/edcyldr.html].

28. Geoffrey Jones, "The Gramophone Company: An Anglo-American Multinational, 1898–1931," *Business History Review*, Spring 1985, p. 79.

29. http://www.giga-usa.com/gigaweb1/quotes2/quautscottcpx001.htm. Scott is the source of another great quote also appropriate for this book, "Comment is free, but facts are sacred."

30. Albert Abramson, *The History of Television: 1880 to 1941* (Jefferson, North Carolina: McFarland, 1987), p. 10.

31. David E. Fisher and Marshall Jon Fisher, *Tube: The Invention of Television* (Washington, D.C.: Counterpoint, 1996), pp. 17–18.

32. Fisher and Fisher, *Tube*, p. 37.

33. George Everson, *The Story of Television: The Life of Philo T. Farnsworth* (New York: Arno Press, 1974 [1949, W.W. Norton]) p. 51.

34. Everson, *The Story of Television*, p. 66.

35. Everson, *The Story of Television*, pp. 114–117.

36. Abramson, *Zworykin, Pioneer of Television* (Urbana, Ill.: University of Illinois Press, 1995), p. xiv.

37. Richard S. Rosenbloom and Karen J. Freeze, "Ampex Corporation and Video Innovation," in *Research on Technological Innovation, Management and Policy*, vol. 2, ed. R. S. Rosenbloom (Greenwich, Conn.: JAI Press, 1985), p. 120.

38. Rosenbloom and Freeze, "Ampex Corporation and Video Innovation," p. 121.

39. Lorna Fernandes, "The Evolution of a Leader: Former Reel-to-Reel Giant Ampex Stakes Its Claim on High End Internet Video for the Future," *San Francisco Business Times*, September 27, 1999.

40. Fernandes, "The Evolution of a Leader," pp. 131–132, citing the *Wall Street Journal*, April 16, 1956, p. 16.

41. Fernandes, "The Evolution of a Leader," p. 131.

42. Fernandes, "The Evolution of a Leader," p. 123.

43. Sections of this text appeared in Robert A. Burgelman and Philip Meza, "Peer-to-Peer Computing: Back to the Future," Stanford Graduate School of Business, 2000, SM-76.

44. A cache (pronounced "cash") offers temporary storage. For example, Web pages are stored in a browser's cache directory on the PC's hard disc. When the user returns to a recently viewed Web page, the browser retrieves the page from its cache rather than the original server, saving the user time and reducing burden on the network.

45. This section is informed by "Peer-to-Peer Technology," *Intel Backgrounder*, August 2000. [www.intel.com].

46. In a network, a node is a connection point, a redistribution point, or an endpoint for data transmissions. In general, a node has programmed or engineered capability to recognize and process or forward transmissions to other nodes. Each computer on a network—such as the Internet—is a node if it is accessible to other computers on the network.

Chapter 3

1. Alvin F. Harlow, *Old Wires and New Waves* (New York: D. Appleton-Century Company, 1936), p. 469.

2. Gleason L. Archer, *History of Radio to 1926* (New York: The American Historical Society, 1938), pp. 112–113.

3. Archer, *History of Radio to 1926,* p. 189.

4. This is similar to the strategy used by Intel today in which the company promotes and subsidizes WiFi and WiMax investments in the hope of building demand for mobile computers containing Intel microprocessors.

5. Tom Lewis, *Empire of the Air* (New York: Edward Burlingame Books, 1991), p. 154.

6. Lewis, *Empire of the Air,* p. 155.

7. Barnouw, *A Tower in Babel: A History of Broadcasting in the United States, Vol. I— to 1933* (New York: Oxford University Press, 1966), pp. 108–113. Interestingly, the anniversary of this milestone was observed by radio host Garrison Keillor in his daily radio show "The Writer's Almanac" on August 28, 2003, when Keillor informed listeners, "On this day in 1922, WEAF in New York aired the first commercial in the history of radio. It was for an apartment complex in the suburbs of New York. H. M. Blackwell, a representative of the Queensboro Corporation, talked for ten minutes about the advantages of living in the suburbs . . . Blackwell talked about the apartments without mentioning anything about the rates. He only mentioned the Queensboro Corporation once by name."

8. Herman S. Hettinger, "Broadcast Advertising in 1938: Retail Radio Sales in the United States, 1922–1938," *Broadcasting and Broadcast Advertising 1939 Yearbook* (New York: Broadcasting Publications, 1939), p. 11.

9. Horace Coon, *American Tel & Tel* (New York: Longmans, Green and Co., 1939), pp. 205–214.

10. Barnouw, *A Tower in Babel,* p. 191.

11. Barnouw, *The Golden Web: A History of Broadcasting in the United States, Volume II—1933–1953* (New York: Oxford University Press, 1968), p. 57.

12. Robert Sobel, *RCA* (New York: Stein and Day, 1986), p. 82.

13. Sobel, *RCA.*

14. Sobel, *RCA,* p. 84.

15. Sobel, *RCA,* p. 85.

16. Joshua Chaffin and Andrew Edgecliffe-Johnson, "Digital Sales provide Note of Optimism for Record Industry," *The Financial Times,* October 4, 2005, p.19.

17. Tim Burt, "The Artist Moves to Centre Stage," *The Financial Times,* November 17, 2004, p. 11.

18. Burt, "The Artist Moves to Centre Stage."

19. This is the average range of recording costs and royalty figures, according to an industry executive.

20. Lest we feel too sorry for those early patrons who paid their nickel and probably had to endure many worn-out prints, today a source of disgruntlement for movie patrons stems from accusations that exhibitors use underpowered bulbs in their projectors

to save money on electricity. And a nickel then, regardless of how you account for inflation, was still worth far less than the price of even matinee admissions today.

21. *United States v. Paramount Pictures, Inc.,* 334 U.S. 131 (1948).

22. Tino Balio, "Introduction," in *Hollywood in the Age of Television,* Tino Balio, ed. (Boston: Unwin Hyman, 1990), p. 3.

23. Balio, "Introduction," p. 15.

24. Benjamin Cha and Kausik Rajgopal, "Digital Distribution in the Music Industry in 2001," Stanford Graduate School of Business, 2001, SM-83.

25. Jennifer Sullivan, "Napster! Music Is for Sharing," *Wired,* Nov. 1, 1999.

26. Cha and Rajgopal, "Digital Distribution in the Music Industry in 2001."

27. Cha and Rajgopal, "Digital Distribution in the Music Industry in 2001."

28. Chris Oakes, "AOL Makes Music Noise," *Wired,* June 1, 1999.

29. M. A. Cusumano, Y. Mylonadis, and R. S. Rosenbloom, "Strategic Maneuvering and Mass-Market Dynamics: The Triumph of VHS Over Beta," *Business History Review,* Spring 1992, *66,* 51–94.

30. Cusumano, Mylonadis, and Rosenbloom, "Strategic Maneuvering and Mass-Market Dynamics," p. 54.

31. In 1991, Matsushita acquired MCA. Four years later, in June 1995, the Seagram Company purchased a majority equity stake in MCA from Matsushita. In 1998, Seagram sold much of Universal's television interests to USA Networks in exchange for equity, gaining 45 percent of USA. In December 2000, Universal was purchased by French conglomerate Vivendi Universal, which was forced to sell the studio (and much else) in the wake of its crushing debt load.

32. Jeffrey H. Rohlfs, *Bandwagon Effects in High-Technology Industries* (Cambridge, Mass.: The MIT Press, 2001), p.95.

33. Lewis, *Empire of the Air,* p. 114.

Chapter 4

1. *Eldred et al. v. Ashcroft,* (01-618) 537 U.S. 186 (2003).

2. Mike Musgrove, "Hollings Proposes Copyright Defense," *The Washington Post,* March 22, 2002, p. E03.

3. For an interesting discussion of the effects of the DCMA, see "Unintended Consequences: Five Years Under the DMCA," a white paper published by the Electronic Freedom Foundation (www.eff.org).

4. Mark Boslet and Carmen Fleetwood, "Onslaught of TV, Movie Content Raises Web Regulation Debate," *Wall Street Journal,* May 17, 2006, p. B3B.

5. See Simon Byers, Lorrie Cranor, Eric Cronin, Dave Kormann, and Patrick Mc-Daniel, "Analysis of Security Vulnerabilities in the Movie Production and Distribution Process," in *Proceedings of the 2003 ACM Workshop on Digital Rights Management,* Washington, D.C., October 27, 2003.

6. Paul Boutin, "Will the Broadcast Flag Break Your TiVo?" *Slate,* November 26, 2003. [http://slate.msn.com/id/2091723].

7. Barnouw, *The Golden Web: A History of Broadcasting in the United States, Volume II—1933–1953* (New York: Oxford University Press, 1968), p. 109.

8. Barnouw, *The Golden Web*, p. 217.

9. For an interesting discussion of James C. Pertillo and his association with Jules Stein of MCA, see Connie Bruck, *When Hollywood Had A King* (New York: Random House, 2003).

10. *White-Smith Music Pub. Co. v. Apollo Co.*, 209 U.S. 1 (1908).

11. *White-Smith Music Pub. Co. v. Apollo Co.*, 209 U.S. 1 (1908).

12. Leonard Allen, "The Battle of Tin Pan Alley," *Harper's Magazine*, August 1940, *181*, p. 516.

13. *Herbert v. Shanley Co.*, 242 U.S. 591 (1917).

14. *Buck v. Jewell-La Salle Realty Co.*, 283 U.S. 191 (1931).

15. Allen, "The Battle of Tin Pan Alley," p. 515.

16. www.bmi.com/library/brochures/historybook/creative.asp.

17. Peter B. Orlik, *Encyclopedia of Radio* (New York, Routledge, 2003).

18. Orlik, *Encyclopedia of Radio*.

19. Allen, "The Battle of Tin Pan Alley," p. 522.

20. Allen, "The Battle of Tin Pan Alley," p. 519.

21. Russell Sanjek and David Sanjek, *American Popular Music Business in the 20th Century* (New York: Oxford University Press, 1991), p. 91.

22. John Ryan, *The Production of Culture in the Music Industry: The ASCAP-BMI Controversy* (Lantham, Md.: University Press of America, 1985), pp. 107–108.

23. Ryan, *The Production of Culture in the Music Industry*, pp. 109–113.

24. Portions of this section come from "A Look at Three Regulatory Forces Influencing Content and Distribution in the Motion Picture and Television Industries," Robert A. Burgelman and Philip Meza, Stanford Graduate School of Business, 2003, SM-105.

25. Robert Conly, "The Promise of Television," *The American Mercury*, July 1944, p. 58.

26. Conly, "The Promise of Television," p. 58.

27. Conly, "The Promise of Television," p. 62.

28. Timothy R. White, "Hollywood's Attempt at Appropriating Television," in *Hollywood in the Age of Television*, Tino Balio, ed. (Boston: Unwin Hyman, 1990), pp. 156–157.

29. Erik Barnouw, *The Golden Web*, p. 308.

30. Wasserman as quoted in the *Los Angeles Times* in 1966, in Bruck, *When Hollywood Had a King*, p. 211.

31. Testimony of Jack Valenti before the Subcommittee on Courts, Civil Liberties, and the Administration of Justice. Ninety-Seventh Congress (Home Recording or Copyrighted Works), April 12, 1982.

32. M. A. Cusumano, Y. Mylonadis, and R. S. Rosenbloom, "Strategic Maneuvering and Mass-Market Dynamics: The Triumph of VHS over Beta," *Business History Review*, Spring 1992, *66*, 51–94.

33. See Justice Stevens's majority opinion in *Sony Corporation of America v. Universal City Studios*, Inc. 464 U.S. 417 (1984).

34. Benny Evangelista, "RIAA Decries Drop in CD Sales," *San Francisco Chronicle,* Sept. 3, 2003.

35. C. M. Christenson, *Innovator's Dilemma* (Cambridge, Mass.: Harvard Business School Press, 1997).

36. "Global Sales of Recorded Music Down 9.2% in the First Half of 2002," IFPI, Oct. 10, 2002.

37. "RIAA Releases Mid-Year Snapshot of Music Industry," RIAA, Aug. 26, 2002.

38. Lewis Fanger and Cecilia Goytisolo O'Reilly, "Universal Music Group in 2003," Stanford Graduate School of Business, 2003, SM-112.

39. Matt Bai, "Hating Hilary," *Wired,* Feb. 2002, 11.02.

40. Statement of Hilary Rosen, the WIPO Copyright Treaties Implementation Act, hearing on H.R. 2281 before the Subcommittee on Telecommunications, Trade, and Consumer Protection, House Committee on Commerce, 105th Congress (1998).

Chapter 5

1. Mason Wiley and Damien Bona, *Inside Oscar: The Unofficial History of the Academy Awards* (New York: Ballantine Books, 1996), p. 229.

2. Kate Bulkley, "DVD Sets Rules for Hollywood," *The Financial Times,* January 23, 2004, p. 12.

3. Russell Sanjek and David Sanjek, *American Popular Music Business in the 20th Century* (New York: Oxford University Press, 1991), p. 155.

4. Sanjek and Sanjek, *American Popular Music Business in the 20th Century,* p. 129.

5. Tino Balio, "Introduction," in *Hollywood in the Age of Television,* Tino Balio, ed. (Boston: Unwin Hyman, 1990), p. 3.

6. David O. Selznick, producer of *Gone With the Wind,* quoted in Connie Bruck, *When Hollywood Had a King* (New York: Random House, 2003), p. 113.

7. Balio, "Introduction," p. 31.

8. Bruck, *When Hollywood Had a King,* p. 176.

9. Bruck, *When Hollywood Had a King,* p. 176.

10. Bruck, *When Hollywood Had a King,* p. 211.

11. Balio, "Introduction," p. 38.

12. James Lardner, *Fast Forward* (New York: W.W. Norton, 1987), pp. 168–202.

13. Lardner, *Fast Forward,* pp. 172–173.

14. Bruce C. Klopfenstein, "The Diffusion of the VCR in the United States," in *The VCR Age: Home Video and Mass Communication,* Mark R. Levy, ed. (Newbury Park, Calif.: Sage, 1989).

15. Julie Holland Mortimer, "The Effects of Revenue-Sharing Contracts on Welfare in Vertically-Separated Markets: Evidence from the Video Rental Industry," January 10, 2001, p. 4. [www.bol.ucla.edu/hollandj].

16. Mortimer, "The Effects of Revenue-Sharing Contracts," p. 4.

17. Mortimer, "The Effects of Revenue-Sharing Contracts," p. 4.

18. Tim Burt, "Hollywood Hails DVD and Video Sales," *Financial Times,* January 9, 2003, p. 20.

19. *Fortnightly Corp. v. United Artists Television, Inc.*, 392 U.S. 390 (1968) and *Teleprompter Corp. v. Columbia Broadcasting System, Inc.*, 415 U.S. 394 (1974).

20. Michele Hilmes, *Hollywood and Broadcasting* (Urbana, Ill.: University of Illinois Press, 1990), p.175

21. "The Digital Music Report 2006," IFPI. [www.ifpi.org/content/library/digital-music-report-2006.pdf].

22. This section has been informed by Lewis Fanger and Cecilia Goytisolo O'Reilly, "Universal Music Group in 2003," Stanford Graduate School of Business, 2003, SM-112.

23. E-mail to author, August 2, 2006.

24. E-mail to author, July 13, 2006.

25. E-mail to author, July 13, 2006.

26. E-mail to author, July 13, 2006.

27. "File-Sharing and CD Burning Remain Steady in 2002," *Ipsos*, February 20, 2003.

28. "File-Sharing and CD Burning Remain Steady in 2002."

29. Lewis Fanger and Cecilia O'Reilly (under the supervision of Robert A. Burgelman and Philip E. Meza), "Universal Music Group in 2003," Stanford Graduate School of Business, 2003, SM-112.

30. Seth Schiesel, "And the Band Played On, Online," *New York Times*, January 22, 2004, p. E1.

31. Felix Oberholzer and Koleman Strumpf, "The Effect of File Sharing on Record Sales: An Empirical Analysis," research paper, March 2004. [www.unc.edu/~cigar/papers/FileSharing_March2004.pdf]

32. Source: Informa Media, cited in Tim Burt, "The Media Business Learns a New Song," *Financial Times*, April 13, 2004, p.8.

33. Stan Liebowitz, "Will MP3 Downloads Annihilate the Record Industry? The Evidence So Far," research paper, June 2003. [www.UTdallas.edu/~liebowit/intprop/records.pdf].

34. Bob Tedeschi, "Web Radio Said to Be Ready for Ads," *New York Times*, March 22, 2004.

35. See Chris Anderson, *The Long Tail: Why the Future of Business Is Selling Less of More* (New York: Hyperion, 2006).

Chapter 6

1. As of December 2005; source: www.oecd.org/document/39/0,2340,en_2649_34225_36459431_1_1_1_1,00.html.

2. Demetri Sevastopulo, "Rocky Road to the U.S.'s Broadband Future," *Financial Times*, December 9, 2003. A new regulatory debate concerning so-called "net neutrality" emerged in 2005 that had the potential for telephone and cable companies joining forces against the likes of online companies such as Google and technology companies such as Microsoft. In a nutshell, consumer advocates, online companies, and some technology companies would like to see the concept of net neutrality enshrined in telecommunications regulations being drawn up in the most sweeping overhaul of such laws since the Telecommunications Deregulation Act of 1996. Telecommunications providers such as

phone and cable companies, and some technology companies that supply them as makers of networking gear, would like telecom providers to have the ability to provide tiered service, for example, giving online companies willing to pay the ability to transfer their data packets faster than other Internet traffic. These opponents of net neutrality say that the added revenue they could receive from services that provide preferential treatment to some data packets could help them pay for building increased broadband access to more consumers. Proponents of net neutrality argue that allowing for preferred service would put newer online companies at a disadvantage and slow innovation in online services.

3. Ethan Smith, "Downloading Music Gets More Expensive," *Wall Street Journal*, April 7, 2004, p. D1.

4. Bob Tedeschi, "Music at Your Fingertips, and a Battle Among Sellers," *New York Times*, December 1, 2003.

5. Staci D. Kramer, "Content's King," *CableWorld*, April 29, 2002.

6. Randall Stross, "Someone Has to Pay for TV. But Who? And How?" *New York Times*, May 7, 2006.

7. A. S. Grove, *Only the Paranoid Survive* (New York: Doubleday, 1996 [1999 edition cited]).

8. Walter S. Mossberg, "Apple's Production Model Makes It an Early Winner in Post-PC Era," *Wall Street Journal*, May 12, 2006, p. 27.

9. Bill Gates and Paul Otellini, "End of the PC Era? Hardly!" *Wall Street Journal*, May 15, 2006.

Appendix A

1. Gordon Moore, Keynote Address: International Solid-State Circuits Conference, San Francisco, February 10, 2003. [www.intel.com/pressroom/archive/speeches/moore20030210.htm].

2. If you are looking at this footnote because you wonder why the group is abbreviated ISO and not IOS, here is what the ISO's Website has to say about it: "Because 'International Organization for Standardization' would have different abbreviations in different languages ('IOS' in English, 'OIN' in French for Organisation internationale de normalisation), it was decided at the outset to use a word derived from the Greek isos, meaning 'equal.' Therefore, whatever the country, whatever the language, the short form of the organization's name is always ISO." [www.iso.org/en/aboutiso/introduction/index.htm].

3. Sam Paltridge, "The Development of Broadband Access in OECD Countries," Organization for Economic Cooperation and Development (OECD), October 29, 2001. [www.oecd.org/pdf/M00020000/M00020255.pdf].

4. An organization that owns two or more cable television systems is known as a multiple system operator (MSO). Prominent examples of MSOs include Comcast, TimeWarner Cable, and Cox Communications.

5. Milo Medin and Jay Rolls, "The Internet Via Cable," *Scientific American*, October 1999, pp. 100–102.

6. Medin and Rolls, "The Internet Via Cable."

7. Asymmetric DSL (ADSL) and Symmetric DSL (SDSL) are the most popular forms of DSL in the world. In addition, other types of DSL include High-data-rate DSL (HDSL) and Very-high-rate DSL (VDSL).

8. George T. Hawley, "Broadband by Phone," *Scientific American,* October 1999, pp. 102–104.

Appendix B

1. Kevin G. Rivette and David Kline, *Rembrandts in the Attic* (Boston: Harvard Business School Press, 1999), p. 5.

2. Press Release, "IIPA Economist Study Reveals Copyright Industries Remain a Driving Force in the U.S. Economy," April 22, 2002. [www.iipa.com].

3. Adrienne Koch and William Peden (eds.), *The Life and Selected Writings of Thomas Jefferson* (New York: Modern Library, 1972), p. 630.

4. Paul Goldstein, *Copyright's Highway* (New York: Hill and Wang, 1994), p. 202.

5. United States Constitution, Article I, Section 8.

6. Some of these models turn up in antique fairs across the country, and have been featured on the PBS television series *Antiques Roadshow.*

7. John Schwartz, "How Low Can DVD Players Go?" *New York Times,* December 7, 2003, p. 5. The article cites Sharp Electronic as the source of price estimates.

8. This section is adapted from Philip Meza and Robert A. Burgelman, "Finding the Balance: Intellectual Property in the Digital Age," Stanford Graduate School of Business, 2003, SM-107.

9. Goldstein, *Copyright's Highway,* p. 202.

10. Charles C. Mann, "The Heavenly Juke Box," *The Atlantic Monthly,* September 2000, pp. 39–59.

11. *NEC Corp. v. Intel Corp.,* 10 U.S.P.Q.2d (BNA) 1177 (N.D. Cal. 1989).

12. *Mitchell Brothers Film Group v. Cinema Adult Theater,* 604 F.2d 852 (5th cer. 1979), cert. Denied, 445 U.S. 917 (1980).

13. See Copyright Act §303.

14. www.chillingeffects.org/copyright/faq.cgi#QID8.

15. 17 U.S.C. §107.

16. *Fox Film Corp. v. Doyal,* 286 U.S. 123, 127 (1932).

17. *United States v. Paramount Pictures, Inc.,* 334 U.S. 131, 158 (1948).

18. *Sony Corp. v. Universal Studios, Inc.,* 464 U.S. 417, 429 (1984).

19. Goldstein, *Copyright's Highway,* p. 172.

INDEX